90 DAYS, 90 WAYS

Inspiration, Tips & Strategies
for Academic Writers

Patricia Goodson, Ph.D.
Mina Beigi, Ph.D.
Melika Shirmohammadi, Ph.D.

2020

Copyright © 2020 by Patricia Goodson, Mina Beigi, Melika Shirmohammadi

All rights reserved. No part of this book may be reproduced or transmitted in any form or by any means electronic or mechanical, including photocopying, recording, or by any information and retrieval storage system, without permission from the authors. For permission, please contact the authors by Email: 90Days90WaysBook@gmail.com

All Cartoons used by permission. Requests for permission should be directed to:
Karen and Christie Glasbergen at Glasbergen Cartoon Service.
E-mail: randy@glasbergen.com
Web: http://www.glasbergen.com

Editor: Erin McTigue, Ph.D. – www.positiveacademic.com

Cover Design: Nasrin Jabbari

ISBN: 9798698139881
Amazon Edition
Published in the United States of America

Dedicated To…

My father, Curtis C. Goodson (1928 – 2020) who, the week before he died, asked *"How's the book going?"* and has always been this book's greatest fan.
Patricia Goodson

Ali Divandari, who inspired me to become an academic, and write, when no one else did.
Mina Beigi

Mina and Pat who fuel my writing soul.
Melika Shirmohammadi

Whenever you are fed up with life, start writing:

Ink is the great cure for all human ills…

C.S. Lewis

TABLE OF CONTENTS

Preface – All About Joy	11
The Authors – All About Us	13

Week 1
Days 01 – 07 15

MONDAY	BOOKS TO READ	Stylish Academic Writing	16
TUESDAY	DEEP PRACTICE	Translating Academic-ish	17
WEDNESDAY	HUMOR	Must-Have Items for Productive Writers	18
THURSDAY	INSPIRATION	Fixed or Growth?	19
FRIDAY	RESEARCH	How Long Does It Take to Form a Habit?	20
SATURDAY	TIPS & TOOLS	Priority Setting	21
SUNDAY	WRITING PROMPTS	Influenced My Writing	22

Week 2
Days 08 – 14 23

MONDAY	BOOKS TO READ	Publish & Flourish: Become a Prolific Scholar - 15th Anniversary Edition	24
TUESDAY	DEEP PRACTICE	Copying Exercise	25
WEDNESDAY	HUMOR	Practicing Rejection	26
THURSDAY	INSPIRATION	A Writer Identity	27
FRIDAY	RESEARCH	Reflections on Ten Years of Teaching Writing for Publication to Graduate Students and Junior Faculty	28
SATURDAY	TIPS & TOOLS	Keep a Writing Journal	29
SUNDAY	WRITING PROMPTS	Social Impact	30

Week 3
Days 15 – 21 — 31

MONDAY	BOOKS TO READ	The Practicing Mind	32
TUESDAY	DEEP PRACTICE	Set A Goal for Your Writing Session	33
WEDNESDAY	HUMOR	Honestly, Reviewers!	34
THURSDAY	INSPIRATION	Your Writing Mission/Vision	35
FRIDAY	RESEARCH	Write On! Through to the PhD: Using Writing Groups To Facilitate Doctoral Degree Progress	36
SATURDAY	TIPS & TOOLS	ProWritingAid	37
SUNDAY	WRITING PROMPTS	Diversity Statement	38

Week 4
Days 22 – 28 — 39

MONDAY	BOOKS TO READ	How to Write A Lot	40
TUESDAY	DEEP PRACTICE	Set Goals for your Semester/Quarter	41
WEDNESDAY	HUMOR	Cartoon	42
THURSDAY	INSPIRATION	If It Works For Others	43
FRIDAY	RESEARCH	A Multicomponent Measure of Writing Motivation	44
SATURDAY	TIPS & TOOLS	Tracking	45
SUNDAY	WRITING PROMPTS	Expressive Writing	46

Week 5
Days 29 – 35 — 47

MONDAY	BOOKS TO READ	The Writer's Daily Companion: 365 Inspirations and Writing Tips	48
TUESDAY	DEEP PRACTICE	Set Monthly, Weekly, and Daily Goals	49
WEDNESDAY	HUMOR	Dear Editor-in-Chief	50

THURSDAY	INSPIRATION	Working Well	51
FRIDAY	RESEARCH	The Neuroscience of Creative Writing	52
SATURDAY	TIPS & TOOLS	Sketch Notes	53
SUNDAY	WRITING PROMPTS	My Favorite	54

Week 6
Days 36 – 42 55

MONDAY	BOOKS TO READ	Journal Keeping: How to Use Reflective Writing for Learning, Teaching, Professional Insight, and Positive Change	56
TUESDAY	DEEP PRACTICE	Slowing Down	57
WEDNESDAY	HUMOR	Dear Google Scholar	58
THURSDAY	INSPIRATION	Writing and Loneliness — Ours and Yours	59
FRIDAY	RESEARCH	It's Always a Pleasure: Exploring Productivity and Pleasure in a Writing Group for Early Career Academics	60
SATURDAY	TIPS & TOOLS	The List	61
SUNDAY	WRITING PROMPTS	Reflecting on Feedback	62

Week 7
Days 43 – 49 63

MONDAY	BOOKS TO READ	Writing to Learn: How to Write — And Think — Clearly About Any Subject At All	64
TUESDAY	DEEP PRACTICE	Capturing Negative Thoughts	65
WEDNESDAY	HUMOR	Attending an International Conference?	66
THURSDAY	INSPIRATION	A Community	67
FRIDAY	RESEARCH	Preventing Choking	68
SATURDAY	TIPS & TOOLS	Textbook and Academic Authors Association - TAA	69
SUNDAY	WRITING PROMPTS	Purpose Statement	70

Week 8
Days 50 – 56 71

MONDAY	BOOKS TO READ	Liberating Scholarly Writing: The Power of Personal Narrative ...	72
TUESDAY	DEEP PRACTICE	The Practice Paradox	73
WEDNESDAY	HUMOR	Cartoon	74
THURSDAY	INSPIRATION	Motivation: When You Have None	75
FRIDAY	RESEARCH	Factors Related to Publication Success	76
SATURDAY	TIPS & TOOLS	Hire an Editor	77
SUNDAY	WRITING PROMPTS	Descriptive Writing	78

Week 9
Days 57 – 63 79

MONDAY	BOOKS TO READ	It Was the Best of Sentences, It Was the Worst of Sentences	80
TUESDAY	DEEP PRACTICE	Practicing DOC	81
WEDNESDAY	HUMOR	Letter from A Journal Reviewer	82
THURSDAY	INSPIRATION	Writing Shoes	83
FRIDAY	RESEARCH	Increasing Writing Self-Efficacy of Adult Learners	84
SATURDAY	TIPS & TOOLS	Daily Steps	85
SUNDAY	WRITING PROMPTS	Reflections on Writing	86

Week 10
Days 64 – 70 87

MONDAY	BOOKS TO READ	A Guide to Publishing for Academics	88
TUESDAY	DEEP PRACTICE	Reading with Purpose	89
WEDNESDAY	HUMOR	A Writing Carol	90
THURSDAY	INSPIRATION	Writing? What's THAT?	91

Friday	Research	Writing Anxiety and Writing Self-Efficacy	92
Saturday	Tips & Tools	Mind Mapping	93
Sunday	Writing Prompts	Reasons Why	94

Week 11

Days 71 – 77 — 95

Monday	Books to Read	The Artist's Way — A Spiritual Path to Higher Creativity	96
Tuesday	Deep Practice	What Is Your System?	97
Wednesday	Humor	Top 10 Tips for Becoming a Terrible Academic Writer	98
Thursday	Inspiration	Writing to Slow Down	99
Friday	Research	Micro-Breaks	100
Saturday	Tips & Tools	Don't Break the Chain	101
Sunday	Writing Prompts	Dear Editor	102

Week 12

Days 78 – 84 — 103

Monday	Books to Read	Becoming an Academic Writer: 50 Exercises for Paced, Productive, and Powerful Writing	104
Tuesday	Deep Practice	Practicing Feedback	105
Wednesday	Humor	Cartoon	106
Thursday	Inspiration	Being Kind to a Rejected Paper	107
Friday	Research	Verbs	108
Saturday	Tips & Tools	Panda Planner	109
Sunday	Writing Prompts	Questioning Assumptions	110

Week 13
Days 85 – 90 111

MONDAY	BOOKS TO READ	Professors as Writers: A Self-Help Guide to Productive Writing	112
TUESDAY	DEEP PRACTICE	A 30-Day Writing Challenge	113
WEDNESDAY	HUMOR	To-Do: A List for Writers Preparing (Not) to Write	114
THURSDAY	INSPIRATION	Accomplishments List	115
FRIDAY	RESEARCH	Writing About Your Goals Works!	116
SATURDAY	TIPS & TOOLS	De-Jargonizer	117

PREFACE

All About Joy

Here is a book for you to read and digest in small bits: One-entry-a-day — with a 90-day supply — much like supplements or vitamins you take for dietary deficiencies. Academics have a steady diet of non-palatable writing, frequently done under stressful circumstances and, more often than not, in total isolation. The diet is strict and harsh; the rewards are few and rare. One needs nourishing supplements before malnutrition sets in.

This book is for *you*, if you see yourself as an academic writer. The label "academic writer" applies if you write within the context of higher education training programs, settings, and/or professional fields; if the bulk of your audience comprises your peers, readers with college/post-graduate degrees, or aspiring degree-seekers.

As an established or upcoming scholar, you are well aware that academic writing is a demanding and arduous task, often done in isolation, within structures that encourage delayed gratification. Even when we don't experience loneliness or aversion, the writing task can often be boring and tedious. The *daunting-ness* of projects as well as the solitary work and the daily grind make it quite a challenge to sustain motivation or momentum.

We wrote this book to help a bit: To motivate, affirm, and entertain — with the goal of sustaining an enjoyable writing habit and decreasing writing stress. If we read, as C.S. Lewis once wrote, "to know we're not alone", daily reading of a short text, written *by* and *for* academic authors, can help nurture the sense that we belong to a community of writers. The text aims at fostering that sense. And, perhaps only modestly, feeling that 'we are not alone' can bring a tad of joy to our routine writing.

We all know how thirsty we are for joy these days…

We designed the text to cover 90 days of entries. Because we do not date them, you can start using the book at any time of the year.

We categorized the entries according to the day of the week on which they fall. See the table on the next page for each day's focus.

Structured in this manner, we hope the book is useful, not merely inspirational, and we would love to hear from you – your comments, suggestions, and questions. In the next few pages, you will find a little blurb about each of us, along with our contact information. So, please stay in touch?

We hope reading this book brings you half the joy we experienced writing it. And, if joy does come to visit… well, invite it to stay awhile…

PREFACE

Mondays — **Books to Read**
Mini-reviews of books that are useful for academic writers because they provide information, motivation, and useful resources.

Tuesdays — **Deep Practice**
To align itself with the perspective taken in Goodson's previous text (Becoming an Academic Writer), this category contains suggestions for exercises to practice different dimensions of the writing process. These entries require the reader to write/practice writing following a prompt. The prompts for practice relate to academic content, exclusively.

Wednesdays — **Humor**
This category contains entertaining texts and mock letters as a way to provide positive emotional support for writers. The goal, here, is entertainment and eliciting of positive emotions related to academic writing. On Weeks 4, 8, and 12 we share a cartoon in place of text. Again, just for fun…

Thursdays — **Inspiration**
This category contains text to inspire and move academic writers to believe they can, in fact, sustain the academic writing task, even if it is arduous.

Fridays — **Research**
Science literature is sparse on research regarding academic writing at the graduate and post-graduate levels, but many of the available findings are useful to sustain writers' motivation and resolve. Writing inquiry also proves useful to validate certain practices (such as developing a writing habit). Academic writers – because many of them conduct their own research – tend to value evidence that supports their actions/behaviors.

Saturdays — **Tips & Tools**
This category also provides instrumental support for authors, in the form of available tools, gadgets, services or suggestions for improving writing quality and quantity.

Sundays — **Writing Prompts**
This category (similar to the Deep Practice one) contains prompts associated with academic texts to help writers begin writing "something"… and then transition into their own writing a bit more easily.

THE AUTHORS

All About Us

We thought you might like to know who we are.

You will see that we refer to ourselves in the entries using our initials: PG, MB, and MS. We worked on the book as a team, but each had our preferences for certain categories, so we divided the work accordingly. You may notice the difference in "voice", across the pieces: Yes, that is intentional. Each of us has a strong and unique voice reflected in our writing and we had no intention to smooth that out and make the text sound as if a single person had written it (even though this is, precisely, what we spend a lot of our time doing, when writing for academic publications in writing teams, right?). Nope. Not here. So, below, is a chance to learn about us, before you hear our voices in our words.

We hope you have fun using this text! And if you do en-*JOY* it, send us a note; share it with others, or write something of your own to celebrate!

Wishing you much joyful writing ahead,

Pat, Mina, and *Melika*
College Station, Texas, USA; Southampton, UK.; Houston, Texas, USA.

Patricia Goodson, Ph.D.
Email: **90Days90WaysBook@gmail.com**

Pat is a Presidential Professor for Teaching Excellence at Texas A&M University (TAMU), in the US. She developed (and directs) a peer-led support service for academic writers at TAMU. The service is known as POWER (where POWER stands for Promoting Outstanding Writing for Excellence in Research). As a result of developing and working with POWER, Pat put together a system/model for writing productivity. This model emphasizes specific strategies, functional tools, and instrumental support for writers. The POWER system/model appears in the book Pat authored, published by SAGE: *Becoming an Academic Writer: 50 Exercises for Paced, Productive, and Powerful Writing.* Pat's scholarly agenda focuses on health promotion. Specifically, sexual health and health education. Recently, she is researching and writing about complex dynamic systems and meta-science.

Pat developed a sustainable writing habit and is thrilled when she sees other writers becoming more productive and less stressed as they try out the strategies she teaches (none of which, by the way, are new—many have been around for quite a while). Pat teaches a writing productivity course to graduate students at TAMU, leads POWER Writing Studios there, too, and facilitates writing productivity workshops for academic groups, nation-wide (and sometimes abroad!). Her writing

THE AUTHORS

happens every weekday, early mornings; she has no social media accounts and only turns her cell phone on when she's travelling (to great annoyance of all her friends).

Mina Beigi, Ph.D.
Email: **90Days90WaysBook@gmail.com**

Mina is an Associate Professor of Organizational Behavior and Human Resource Management at the University of Southampton, in the UK. Mina has always had a passion for stories and writing; she transitioned from a quantitative researcher to a qualitative researcher (yes; after getting a second Ph.D. degree!) to be more engaged with stories and writing in her research and academic life. She took Pat Goodson's writing productivity course, shifted from a binge writer to a writer with healthy writing habits (most of the time!), and worked as a POWER consultant at TAMU from 2013 to 2015. She tries to transfer what she has gained from her academic writing journey to graduate students and peers whenever possible.

Mina studies work-nonwork interface, career success, and understudied careers using in-depth qualitative methodologies. She strives to uncover unexplored career trajectories. In particular, she is interested in theorizing about the role of understudied contexts in the way individuals navigate their careers, as they combine their personal and professional lives. Mina's research informs individuals who take ownership of their careers and helps organizations learn more about their employees' work and nonwork needs.

Melika Shirmohammadi, Ph.D.
Email: **90Days90WaysBook@gmail.com**

Melika is an Assistant Professor of Human Resource Development at the University of Houston, in the US. She is curious about the role of work in people's lives and interested in research questions about how workers from understudied backgrounds navigate their careers and integrate their work and nonwork domains.

Melika earned her Ph.D. in 2018 from Texas A&M University, where she worked for four years as a graduate assistant for POWER. At first, Melika was the recipient of POWER's training and support; later, she became the provider of that training and support, volunteering as a writing consultant and workshop instructor. Melika's engagement with POWER led to an epiphany—"You are an academic 'writer'!"—which made her realize writing is her craft and is *essential* to success in academia. Upon this realization, she has embraced the notion that writing is a process and a continuous practice! She writes regularly and… get this: Even enjoys it!

WEEK 1
Days 01 - 07

"I work 12 hours a day, I exercise 7 days a week, I prepare healthy meals at home instead of going out and it's all paying off. I'm finally too tired to care about being perfect!"

MONDAY
Week 1 - BOOKS TO READ

Stylish Academic Writing

Helen Sword's[1] book is a favorite! Unlike other texts in the academic writing genre, she does not teach how to be more productive, nor provides tips for dealing with thorny portions of text. She addresses, instead, the topics of… (ready for this?): Beauty and style in academic writing. Yes, you read correctly: B-E-A-U-T-Y…

Sword raises the question few people dare ask, right there in Chapter 1: "Pick up a peer-reviewed journal in just about any academic discipline and what will you find? Impersonal, stodgy, jargon-laden, abstract prose …" And she nails it: "There is a massive gap between what most readers consider to be good writing and what academics typically produce and publish. I'm not talking about the kinds of formal strictures necessarily imposed by journal editors—article length, citation style, and the like—but about a deeper, duller kind of disciplinary monotony, a compulsive proclivity for discursive obscurantism and circumambulatory diction (translation: An addiction to big words and soggy syntax)" (p. 3).

Sword's main point is this: Academic writing does not have to be dull, tiresome or lifeless. A writer who pays attention, devotes time to careful editing, and seeks feedback on his/her writing systematically, can write material that readers desire to read (as opposed to feel obligated to read, merely to be informed).

Reading Sword's book leads to examining our writing more carefully while motivating us to "push" for both elegance and precision. She entices readers/writers to aim for the "wow!" factor when writing, with suggestions gleaned from the study of 500 scholarly publications in various fields/disciplines. The book is worth reading. If nothing else, merely to savor Sword's elegant style — and that, alone, can resurrect our writing from its dullness.

---

[1] Sword, Helen. (2012). **Stylish Academic Writing**. Harvard University Press.

TUESDAY
Week 1 - DEEP PRACTICE

Translating Academic-ish

You may have struggled to master academic English (or Academic-ish) but now you write in a competent manner. Reviewers consider it acceptable; you have, after all, managed to publish a few articles already.

Yet mastering Academic-ish may not be enough to communicate the story about your research or your scholarship to non-academics who might benefit from your work. You may also need to take your findings to the general public and to academics outside your field. In other words, you need to communicate your research in non-jargon language.

Today, then, try your hand at writing about one main finding from your research, in non-Academic-ish. Remember: This requires practice. Do it slowly and pay attention. Focus on only one finding. Translate the jargon-laid language into everyday English. To help, imagine yourself as an investigative journalist, trying to tell the story of your work to the lay public.

If beginning with your own research seems too daunting, try translating the segment below, into non-jargony-language and see how well you do (if the terminology here is unfamiliar to you, choose a journal article in your own field). To optimize the practice, obtain feedback from a lay (not academic) person. Ask what he/she "gets" out of reading your text.

Here's a sample to begin practicing: "As mentioned previously, eight of the reviewed studies investigated the relationship between drinking alcohol and friendship networks (drinking frequency and amount of drinking). For instance, the study conducted by Fujimoto and Valente (2012a) examined the influence of friendship types on adolescents' substance use, including drinking (frequency). Authors classified three types of friendships: Mutual friendships, directional friendships, and intimate friendships (…). A mutual friendship was defined as reciprocated friends (knowing each other as friends). A directional friendship was defined as an unreciprocated nomination that originated either from an ego or from an alter (i.e., ego-nominating friend and alter-nominating friend). An intimate friendship was defined as closest or best friends who were being first nominated (…)."[2]

Your translation could begin with, "As we said, in eight articles we read, researchers explored whether an adolescent's group of friends had anything to do with that adolescent drinking alcohol. In other words: Do teenagers follow the behavior of their group?"

Give it a try!

---

[2] Jeon, K.C. & Goodson, P. (2015). US adolescents' friendship networks and health risk behaviors: a systematic review of studies using social network analysis and Add Health data. *PeerJ* 3:e1052; DOI 10.7717/peerj.1052, p. 17/29. Available: https://pubmed.ncbi.nlm.nih.gov/26157622/

WEDNESDAY
Week 1 - HUMOR

Must-Have Items for Productive Writers

- ☑ Adult version of a chair harness/strap — to remind you (gently) to stay seated every time you're tempted to get up and check whether you are needed somewhere else.
- ☑ 45-min sand clock together with a mobile phone locker — to deprive the virtual world — especially Social Media— from your invaluable contributions for at least three quarters of an hour (yes… their loss!).
- ☑ Two sets of clothes at least two sizes bigger than your own — to fool you into believing you are super fit and there is no need to worry about your weight.
- ☑ A fan, a space heater, and a robot vacuum cleaner — to bypass the major weather or cleaning-related excuses for not writing today.
- ☑ A copy of the first paragraph from the feedback you received from anonymous journal reviewers — right before they begin using words such as "but" or "however" when reviewing your article — to be tacked to the wall in front of your desk to remind you how awesome you are and that you're still in the game.
- ☑ A framed photo of the most miserable holiday you ever took — to help you maintain perspective: Sitting (or standing) in front of a monitor and typing one sentence after another is not the worst thing in the world, after all!
- ☑ Miniature pictures of broccoli, cabbage, Brussels sprouts, kale, turnip, asparagus, and celery —to remind you it's not worth interrupting your writing to check what's in the fridge.

THURSDAY
Week 1 - INSPIRATION

Fixed or Growth?

Carol S. Dweck[3], in her book "Mindset: The New Psychology of Success" describes two mindsets. One, she calls "fixed". People who have this mindset believe they either do or do not have a specific talent. The other, she calls a "growth mindset". People with this perspective believe they can become good at a task, by learning and practicing.

These two groups view effort, practice, and hard work in diametrically opposite ways. Fixed mindset people view effort and practice as something for "those who can't make it on talent" (p. 44). Growth mindset folks, however, believe in the "transformative power of effort" and are constantly creating new ways of learning and practicing. Even more, those with a growth mindset see value in the process, not merely in the outcome; they enjoy learning, practicing, and growing. People with a growth mindset value effort and practice; fixed mindset folks, scorn them.

So… which mindset do you have about academic writing? If you think "I'm not a good writer" or, simply, "I'm not a writer", you probably have a fixed mindset. If you think, "I wonder if I can do this?" or "I know if I practice enough, I can only get better!", then you have a growth mindset. Which one characterizes you at this moment? (no doubt, the answer may depend on what kind of a day you've been having…).

Take a few moments to craft a paragraph reflecting on this. Be honest.

If you identify yourself as having a fixed mindset, try not to entrench yourself in a fixed mindset about having a fixed mindset… I know, this sentence sounded awful, but it addresses an important logic step. Believing you can change your mindset is the first step in changing; believing you cannot change, fixes you in a certain place/belief. In the coming week, observe people around you, especially people whom you see as having a growth mindset. Seek them out, talk about your desire to change (assuming you really do want a more helpful perspective), ask for suggestions. By doing this, you will have begun to shape your view of your academic writing practice and of yourself as a writer, into a healthier, more positive image.

---

[3] Dweck, C. (2006). **Mindset: The New Psychology of Success**. Random House.

FRIDAY
Week 1 - RESEARCH

How Long Does It Take to Form a Habit?

Researchers at University College London, in the UK, conducted a study to investigate how people develop habits[4]. One hypothesis they tested was that the relationship between the number of repetitions of a behavior/task is not linearly associated with establishing a habit. In other words, more repetitions don't translate into more automaticity, only maintain the established habit. More interesting, however, was the answer the question "How long does it take to form a habit?" – something on the mind of most writers, when challenged to develop a consistent writing habit.

Close to 100 (n= 96) graduate students (30 men and 66 women) participated in this study. Each volunteer participant had to choose a behavior related to healthy eating (27 chose this), drinking (31) or exercise (34); 4 people chose meditation as the behavior they wanted to practice. They were instructed to perform the behavior, daily, for 84 days. They also had to report daily.

Researchers found that, indeed, the non-linear models showed a better fit than the linear ones, when depicting the relationship between repetition and habit development. At a certain point, repeating a behavior does not increase its automaticity (which may not come as a surprise if you think of certain habits such as toothbrushing). Regarding the "How long does it take?" question, researchers observed the median number of repetitions needed to reach a plateau level of habit was 66 days (ranging between 18 and 254).

The authors concluded:

… It can take a large number of repetitions for an individual to reach their highest level of automaticity for some behaviors, and therefore creating new habits will require self-control to be maintained for a significant period before the desired behaviors acquire the necessary automaticity to be performed without self-control. (p. 1008)

The take-home message? Don't feel discouraged if you haven't yet established a writing habit that is so automatic, you can't even recall if you had a writing session earlier today or not. Once the habit becomes automatic, you will have to stop for a second and recall whether you wrote that day or not. Until it's that automatic, however, it takes time. Moreover, for some people it takes longer than for others (the time needed also relates to the complexity of the habit).

Keep up the effort to establish your writing habit and, if you already have reached a certain level of automaticity, find other challenges to take on! Keep at it – one healthy habit at a time…

---

[4] Lally, P., Van Jaarsveld, C.H.M., Potts, H.W.W., Wardle, J. (2010). How are habits formed: Modelling habit formation in the real world. European *Journal of Social Psychology, 40,* 998-1009. Available: https://doi.org/10.1002/ejsp.674

SATURDAY
Week 1 - TIPS & TOOLS

Priority Setting

I (PG) struggled for a long time with prioritizing tasks. The difficulty related to my inability to figure out which tasks were the real priority, among a list where all items were both important and urgent. In fact, did you know that legitimate use of the plural form of the word "priority" — "priorities" — is a rather recent cultural phenomenon? Yep: Until recently, the word "priority" was used only in the singular (makes sense if you think about its meaning, doesn't it?).

I tried various strategies to learn how to prioritize, including Stephen Covey's First Things First[5]. None of the systems I tried worked, however, because of this simple issue: Can someone please tell me what is more important on my list of all-important and always (seemingly) urgent to-dos?

Then I learned about the VAST list. And *that* list has made all the difference! (For a more detailed description, see Susan Robison's book, *The Peak Performing Professor*[6], page 100).

You start by listing 3 tasks that, done today, will contribute to your long-term Vision or mission in life. Then you list 3 tasks that — if not done today — will be the end of the world as you know it; in other words, 3 tasks that will help Avert or Avoid disaster. Next come 3 actions that focus on your Self – many times mine are simply, "eat dinner", "get to sleep earlier". Finally, 3 tasks from Tomorrow's list, if you have a fabulous day and are able to get to everything on your list with time to spare.

This system operates on a healthy assumption: There are a finite number of hours in each day – and because no one can manage time, there's nothing we can do about it. Some things will not get done today, no matter what. But the VAST list forces me to choose 9 tasks that will get done today, regardless – and, given the crazy-busy agendas we all have, 9 completed tasks are better than 0 completed tasks, any time, any day.

Give it a try!

---

[5] Covey, S.R. (1996). **First Things First.** Reprint Edition. Free Press.
[6] Robison, S. (2013). **The Peak Performing Professor: A Practical Guide to Productivity and Happiness**. San Francisco, CA. Jossey-Bass.

SUNDAY
Week 1 - WRITING PROMPTS

Influenced My Writing

Helen Sword's book, "Air & Light & Time & Space"[7] calls academic writers to reflect on their academic writing history. Based on her suggestion, today's prompt will allow you to spend a few minutes reflecting on your academic writing life, recalling the authors responsible for shaping your writing as it is, today.

Set your timer for 10 or 15 minutes. In one or two pages, capture the thoughts related to this statement (after filling in the blanks):

> Among the authors/people who most influenced my academic writing was [BLANK], because he/she [BLANK].

And this:

If these people are still alive, consider sending them a note, sharing what you wrote today. It will make their day (and probably yours, too)!!!

---

[7] Sword, H. (2017). **Air & Light & Time & Space: How Successful Academics Write**. Harvard University Press.

WEEK 2
Days 08 – 14

MONDAY
Week 2 - BOOKS TO READ

Publish & Flourish: Become a Prolific Scholar

Tara Gray, author of "Publish & Flourish"[8], is the scholar who ushered me (PG) to a system for writing. Learning and adapting that system led to my authoring a book for academic writers and to creating a peer-support writing service at Texas A&M University, known as P.O.W.E.R. Services. Tara gave me the gift of a system for writing productively, along with clues regarding how the system worked. She is one of the main reasons you are reading this book, right now!

In her book, Tara provides strategies, tips and tools for becoming a prolific scholar. At this point, not many of these strategies are completely new, but Tara's approach to writing, overall, is rather unique. While many writing scholars propose one needs to complete all their research and know What they want to say before beginning the writing process, Tara is among the scholars who say: "Don't wait to start writing until you finish the research… Streamline your research by writing – informally – throughout the project" (p. 30). For some, such writing could be classified as "pre-writing", and it really doesn't "count" as "real writing". But for many of us, finding our way through the formulation of research hypothesis, through the collecting and collating of data, through the analyses and interpretation processes — all this can be done more efficiently by writing. The writing can serve as guideposts along these processes.

Another under-utilized strategy she proposes is to organize one's writing around key sentences and using these key sentences in a reverse-outline of sorts. She is blunt: "Readers expect nonfiction to have one point per paragraph. Ideally, the point of the paragraph should be suggested in one sentence, a key or topic sentence, located early in the paragraph and supported by the rest of the paragraph" (p. 43). This principle is key to organizing a text within a coherent and cohesive structure. If we pay attention to our paragraphs, ensure they only address one key point, and later check a list of key sentences (removed from the text by copying-and-pasting them into a separate file), we can check whether the text is ordered in some fashion, whether it flows from one idea to another or whether there are gaps and jumps between key ideas. This notion of reverse outlining may well be one of the most useful contributions Tara Gray makes in her book.

Aside from tips on creating a writing habit, generating text quickly, and editing efficiently, Tara provides suggestions for how to conduct useful writing group meetings, how to solicit feedback on your writing from experts "with a capital E" (with a sample email asking for such feedback) and supports her strategies with data she has collected through the years. All of this, along with a writing style that is vibrant, crisp, and uplifting.

She will get you writing – the book you are now reading is living proof!

---

[8] Gray, T. (2020). **Publish & Flourish: Become a Prolific Scholar**. 15th Anniversary Kindle Edition.

TUESDAY
Week 2 - DEEP PRACTICE

Copying Exercise

For any other skill we wish to learn or perfect, we will be directed to follow models: Listen to specific recordings of someone playing the guitar, watch videos of someone playing tennis, watch glassblowers molding beautiful vases. Why, then, are we never instructed to follow specific models, when writing?

In writing, too, emulating someone else's performance can contribute significantly to enhancing ours.

The fear — as we understand it — has to do with concerns about plagiarism. Yet, even if someone who, while learning to play classical guitar, plays very much like Andres Segovia, we know the apprentice is not claiming to have composed the piece written by Segovia. When he/she plays, the audience will be informed that the musical scores being performed were composed by others. The performer just happens to try to play like the masters! The performer has a goal, a standard to reach, when practicing: To play like Segovia.

The same ideas apply to writing: As academic writers we should have standards or writing we wish to emulate (PG always says, "I want to write like C.S. Lewis, when I grow up!"). When copying, we are practicing using imitation as a technique; we don't claim the words we're copying are ours, in any way. If we wish to use those words in our own writing, we let the readers know they are not our words but were borrowed. Therefore, copying as a form of deep practice in writing is an excellent investment of your time.

Here's how to start: Choose a piece of writing that you consider "stellar". Something authored by someone whom you "wish to be like" when you and your writing grow up. Then, very, very slowly (even by hand, if you can), copy one or two paragraphs of that piece. But the trick is to do this very s-l-o-w-l-y, so your hands and your brain, your whole body in fact, can have time to swallow the style, to embody that way of wording a text. Over time, if you repeat this practice regularly, you will notice subtle changes in your own writing, as you begin to imitate the model.

This strategy is for practice only. Remember: Plagiarism is the intent of passing on someone else's words as your own words. You are copying merely for practice, here. Give it a try: Copy one or two paragraphs as part of your warm-up before your writing.

A tiny investment with huge rewards over time. Try it!

WEDNESDAY

Week 2 - HUMOR

Practicing Rejection

A few years ago, two of us (MB. & MS) submitted a paper to an international conference we really wanted to attend. The conference required submission of a full paper, not merely a proposal or an abstract. We knew the competition was stiff: The chances of having that paper accepted was ridiculously small, and we were working against a tight deadline.

We tried, anyway. As we have learned how important it is to develop a healthy growth-mindset, and to view opportunities such as that conference as a chance to practice writing and receiving feedback, nothing could stop us. We wrote the paper and submitted.

But it wasn't easy: Did we mention working against a tight deadline and being upset that we wouldn't have enough time to polish it as much as we would like? At one point, our anxiety was so strong, it was slowing us down. That's when I (MB) decided to stop and write ourselves a rejection letter.

With that letter, we achieved two important goals: We laughed so hard that we released a lot of our self-imposed pressure and anxiety, AND we practiced being rejected. The practice, we knew, would remove the sting that might come later. Here's what we wrote:

Dear authors,

We are writing to announce that, unfortunately, your paper titled "Blah Blah Blah" has not been short-listed for our upcoming Annual Meeting, in Australia. We received 1,000,000 papers, and due to the extensive pool of papers, we rejected yours. Please do not feel discouraged and don't forget to pay for the conference registration and your annual membership dues, anyway. We will send you, as a member, our high-impact print journals as a monthly reminder of your failure. You may lack competence to present a paper, but we will allow you to attend the conference and even enjoy the free hallway networking.

Looking forward to rejecting you next year, yet again, we remain eager,

The Conference Organizing Team

After much laughter and fun crafting this note, we waited for the verdict. To our surprise, the paper was accepted! Had it not been, though, we were prepared to deal with rejection. Are you?

Just for fun today, draft a rejection email for your most recent submission… and remember that academic writers need to become "practiced" in being rejected!

THURSDAY
Week 2 - INSPIRATION

A Writer Identity

Many of the students who take my (PG) writing productivity course at the university tell me, later, one specific element of the course was a game-changer for them. That element? Viewing themselves as professional writers. Adopting the identity of a writer. Saying to themselves, "I am a writer —whether I have published already, or not."

Do you identify yourself as a writer? When was the last time someone asked you what you did for a living, you answered with: "I am an academic writer." Have you ever said that to others? To yourself?

If you are an academic, you are a WRITER, regardless of your other tasks and roles. You write for a living. Writing is THE main factor upon which your professional success will depend—your promotions, the dissemination of your scholarship, the changes you will make to your field of study. Even if you "only" teach, and don't do any research, keep this in mind: Designing courses, preparing and delivering classes involves much writing—most of which does not end up in print or bound between the covers of a book, but writing, nonetheless.

So… how do you identify yourself? If you are writing in academia, but don't see yourself as a professional writer, why not?

Today, in 150 words or less, write an answer to the question above. If you do see yourself as a writer, reflect on that identity: What does it mean, to you, that you are a PROFESSIONAL WRITER?

FRIDAY
Week 2 - RESEARCH

Reflections on Ten Years of Teaching Writing for Publication To Graduate Students and Junior Faculty [9]

My students (PG's) know Wendy Belcher as the author of the book "*Writing your Journal Article in 12 Weeks*" (SAGE Publications). Hundreds of other students know her as the professor who created and taught a writing course at UCLA which, most likely, saved many academic careers (the course, that is).

In the article "*Reflections on Ten Years of Teaching…*", Belcher details the "origins, pedagogy, structure, and limitations" of that course (begun in 1998 as a workshop). We learn a bit about Belcher and her students' struggles with academic writing, and find our own battles validated with honor: Despite having been an accomplished author before entering graduate school for her Master's, Belcher admits "I couldn't identify how exactly an academic paper was supposed to differ from other types of writing I had learned to do." Being tasked with teaching a writing course to working professionals introduced her to "an entire field … devoted to studying the way people write". (p. 187). Especially touched by Robert Boice's research on academics as writers[10], Belcher began successfully teaching her course and three years later, she returned to graduate school to complete a PhD in English literature.

The assumptions underlying her course are excellent reminders of what we and our colleagues have faced (or are facing) regarding academic writing:

Academic writing instruction is absent from most graduate training programs.

Academics do not openly discuss the writing *process* with colleagues.

Most academics develop a pattern of binge writing and procrastinating until deadlines as their main writing habit.

Much of the instruction graduate students receive regarding academic writing focuses on micro aspects of writing (e.g., grammar, referencing styles) and neglect the macro elements (e.g., crafting an argument; structuring a conceptual paper).

As a result of the course and her book, Belcher became well-known and respected as a writing scholar, yet she candidly claims to have struggled quite a bit with academic writing – and admitted that struggle to her students. For Belcher, it was precisely this admission that sparked much of her success:

"… revealing my own struggles with writing has been at the heart of not only my successful course, which has helped so many to become published writers, but also my own success in becoming a better writer. Some write consistently and well without having to talk about it; most of us need to admit our struggles if we are to move beyond them. <u>If you are one of those people, take heart</u>" (p. 190, emphasis ours).

---

[9] Belcher, W. (2009). Reflections on Ten Years of Teaching Writing for Publication To Graduate Students and Junior Faculty. *Journal of Scholarly Publishing, 40* (2), 184-199. Available: https://www.utpjournals.press/doi/abs/10.3138/jsp.40.2.184

[10] Boice, R.(1990). **Professors as Writers: A Self-Help Guide to Productive Writing**. New Forums Press.

SATURDAY
Week 2 - TIPS & TOOLS

Keep a Writing Journal

No, we're not talking about keeping a personal journal – although we strongly believe in journaling for personal and professional growth (if interested, Stevens and Copper wrote an excellent book about the topic[11]).

Here, we have in mind keeping *a journal for each writing project*. This is something we have done for a long time and are so grateful it is an automatic habit. More than once, our journals have come to our rescue, reminding us of *'what was I thinking?'* at certain moments or stages of a writing project. By the way, it is also a good idea to keep a journal for each data analysis project.

In these journals you don't have to write a lot: Just enough to help:

a) Set a goal for that writing session

b) Note any decisions that should be captured, which won't show up in the writing project itself (for example: "*I have decided to use this structure for my paper, because I read it in so-and-so's article and really think it's helpful; note: Remember to give credit for the structure to that author, in the final version*".)

c) Note where to begin working in the *next session*. This note (a bullet list of no more than 2 or 3 points) is worth the whole practice of journaling. Seeing what we need to do next, each time we open that journal, gives us a starting point for the writing session. No need to wonder or spend time 'getting into' that project again.

This practice of journaling each of your writing projects will help you tame 'writer's block', when beginning a writing session, because you will know where to start (even if you don't remember all the details of that piece). By leaving yourself very specific instructions on what to do next, and simply by following one of those steps, you'll quickly re-immerse yourself in the project, even if you've been away from it for a long time.

Go ahead: Give it a try!

---

[11] Stevens, D., Cooper, J.E. (2009). **Journal Keeping: How to Use Reflective Writing for Learning, Teaching, Professional Insight and Positive Change**. Stylus Publishing.

SUNDAY
Week 2 - WRITING PROMPTS

Social Impact

Researchers writing grant proposals for funding are asked to include a section explaining the contribution their study makes to society. In other words, given the research will be funded by tax-payers' money, how does the knowledge gained from the project benefit them or their descendants?

Many researchers struggle with this portion of the proposal writing, because their projects do not impact society either directly or immediately. Researchers studying social problems, health or education have a much easier time than mathematicians or physicists.

Yet the same line of thinking applies to almost any type of academic writing: Journal articles, books, conference presentations — all of these require the author (you) to explain why (and how) you believe what you wrote adds any value to the on-going conversations about your topic.

Regardless of your discipline, today write a brief text describing, as succinctly as possible (100 words or less) how the research project you are now working on, or the classes you now teach, or the journal article you are now drafting, impact society at a broader level.

Force yourself to think beyond the immediate audience of your peers (those who will review the proposal, attend the class, read your article). Think much broader: How does your writing benefit the big picture of human (or animal) life on this planet? What improvements does it foster? What good (benefit) does it generate?

If you cannot come up with any reasonable explanation, pretend you are writing science-fiction or fantasy: How would your writing make any difference in a galaxy far, far away…? In a place where time stands still… In a world that is not broken by evil…

And if you cannot think of absolutely *any contribution*, perhaps take a break; invite a colleague for a cup of coffee/tea and begin the conversation… Who knows if that shared beverage isn't, already, the beginnings of a meaningful contribution?

WEEK 3
Days 15 - 21

"If you write down your Top 10 goals 1,000 times a day, you can accomplish *anything*...if you have any time left over."

MONDAY
Week 3 - BOOKS TO READ

The Practicing Mind

This book is a gem! Thomas M. Sterner[12] uses the varied dimensions of his professional life — he trained as a jazz pianist and worked many years restoring as well as tuning pianos for big music concerts — to teach readers how to enjoy their work. His perspective focuses on deep or deliberate practice — a special type of practice that pursues the goal of progress or improvement, intentionally[13].

Sterner provides valuable insight not only regarding the joy available in the process of engaging in repetitive, tedious tasks, but also regarding the value of using writing for personal and professional growth. One example he gives of the latter relates to his attempt to learn golf. He talks about how he would make time to practice what he learned in a given training session, then would write about it "in a small journal". "I made sure", he writes, that I wrote a description of everything we had covered in class." He made it a habit of listing what he wished to cover/do during a particular practice session and would ensure that what he did focus on during the session revolved around the process of learning certain aspects of golf, not the outcome. He is quick to remind readers that he didn't put in more than one hour of practice a day, yet his progress stood out among his peers, noticed even by his instructor.

Sterner's book is, therefore, very useful for academic writers – especially for those who hate the process of writing, itself, and do it only to crank out the required publications. Sterner will, very gently, try to convince these writers that one can, in fact, enjoy the process of improving, while engaged in it.

Sterner's recommendations to make "staying in the process as easy as possible" center on what he calls "the four 'S' words": Simplify, small, short, and slow.

You will need to read the book, to learn what he says about each technique (he refers to these four terms as techniques), but it is comforting to know someone has distilled the notion of deep practice in a way writers can relate to. Unfortunately, there is not much out there in terms of resources approaching writing as a developmental process for which deep or deliberate practice is the key to sustained productivity. This book, therefore, is not only a gem, but a rare one. Check it out.

---

[12] Sterner, T.M. (2012). **The Practicing Mind: Developing Focus and Discipline in Your Life.** New World Library.

[13] If you are not familiar with the notion of deep or deliberate practice applied to academic writing, check out my (PG) book, **Becoming an Academic Writer: 50 Exercises for Paced, Productive, and Powerful Writing** – 2nd edition published by SAGE Publications in 2016.

TUESDAY
Week 3 - DEEP PRACTICE

Set A Goal for Your Writing Session

One feature that distinguishes deep practice from other types of practice is this: Deep practice is structured around a specific, achievable goal[14]. Each practice session attempts to achieve a goal. If you wish to adopt deep or deliberate practice for your academic writing, you should structure your writing sessions around a specific goal.

Goals for writing sessions can be outcome-oriented goals — write 1,000 words today, or edit the text down to the word limit imposed by the journal by cutting 500 words. The goals can also be process-oriented goals — build up the time devoted to my writing session, by adding five more minutes to the session, each day this week, or use the copying exercise to fine-tune my style for writing grant proposals.

I (PG) set a goal for each of the projects I work on, before starting each writing session. In my journal for that project, I jot down today's date and write: "Today I want to do X". I try to ensure that X is easy to identify and measure, at the end of my session. I want to be able to come back to my journal, after having worked on my writing and say, "I was able to do X" or, if needed, write "I was only able to do this portion of X. Will need to leave the other portion for tomorrow's session, because it involves finding support for concept A."

It is always helpful to note the reason for not having achieved a specific goal during that particular session. Such reflection can help you become better at goal-setting and will provide data about yourself as a writer — your thinking, decision-making, and behavior patterns.

---

[14] Coyle, D. (2010). **The Talent Code: Greatness Isn't Born. It's Grown. Here's How.** 2nd edition. Arrow Books Ltd.

WEDNESDAY

Week 3 - HUMOR

Honestly, Reviewers!

The table below contains excerpts from a lengthy 10-page response-to-reviewers document. All humor aside: Yes, we do recommend using this format to respond to reviewers. No, we do NOT recommend using the sarcastic tone…

Comment Number	Reviewer ID & Reviewer Comment*[15]	Authors' Response
5.	**Reviewer 1** If we can look at existing publications and arrive at identical conclusions about [this topic], then why does this study need to be published?	Thank you for this timely feedback. This study needs to be published because it has received 12 rejections in the last year. These rejections have resulted in serious depression on our part; when depressed, we eat inordinate amounts of food. Therefore, publishing this article (a) decreases wasting valuable food resources; (b) opens up my therapist's schedule for other academics who might need her; and (c) helps shut up colleagues who love to come by and see if I have "any good news", because it just so happens they received another acceptance letter the night before…
35.	**Reviewer 2** The literature review is unbalanced, heavily favoring [a specific field's] literature. There are many studies outside that literature, conceptually relevant to this study. The manuscript would be stronger if the author(s) used a more even-handed approach to covering the relevant literature.	Because we agree, entirely, with the reviewer's comment, in the revised version of the manuscript we added a footnote stating: "This manuscript would be stronger if the author(s) used a more even-handed approach to covering the relevant literature". We have opted, nonetheless, to presenting a "strong" (and not "stronger") manuscript because balancing this "unbalanced" literature review requires writing a minimum of 255 new pages on the topic. Given the topic's importance, however, we are currently negotiating the publication of a textbook. Thank you for the suggestion!
55.	**Reviewer 3** I was excited to read this paper and think the authors have the opportunity to make a meaningful contribution to the literature; however, I feel the data need some more massaging and packaging to fulfill their potential.	We appreciate this positive feedback. To address this comment, we have now printed all 785 pages of interview transcripts, soaked them in water for three consecutive nights, massaged them for seven hours, and packed them as data cubes that are on their way to the journal's office. Please feel free to use these data cubes in any way you believe might lead to their 'fulfilling their potential'. As the authors we believe, however, that writing up the stories these data tell us *is*, indeed, using the data to their maximum potential.

---

[15] Comments sent by anonymous reviewers from a professional academic journal.

THURSDAY
Week 3 - INSPIRATION

Your Writing Mission/Vision

Mission or vision statements were all the "fad" during the 80's and 90's. Many organizations and industries promoted employees' retreats and set out to collectively write their vision or mission statements. Based on those statements, they went on to develop strategies for achieving what they had envisioned.

So… What is *your* vision for your writing? What *mission* do you have for you as a writer, and for your writing as well? What do you want your writing to achieve? Where do you want your writing to take you? Take a few minutes to reflect about these questions.

Begin, then, drafting a mission/vision statement for your writing. Try keeping it to 50 words or less — doing so will make it easier to recall and mention to others.

Here is my (PG) vision statement — at the time I wrote this book. I have learned that, over time, my vision changes.

>As a writer, I am a reformer, a protester, a protestant.
>My mission is to seduce readers to:
>Consider alternative viewpoints,
>Question the status quo, and
>Search for transformative truth.

What is *your* vision/mission as a writer?

FRIDAY
Week 3 - RESEARCH

Write On! Through to the PhD: Using Writing Groups To Facilitate Doctoral Degree Progress [16]

Recipients of a doctoral degree from a Higher Education Administration program, in a US College of Education, found regular participation in a writing group significantly effective in their progress toward degree completion. Participants reported not only increased scholarly productivity but also emotional benefits such as feeling supported and connected to a community.

Students scheduled a day-long writing session each month and voluntarily attended. Informally held in faculty members' or doctoral students' homes, monthly "Write On!" sessions settled into a routine. Attendance ranged from three to ten participants but continued regularly with participants arriving prepared for a full day dedicated to writing. Additionally, volunteers offered a shorter version of the writing sessions (2-3 hours) called 'MiniWrite!' throughout the academic year in the library, on a weeknight, for students who lived or worked close to the main campus.

"Write On!" sessions represented a dedicated, uninterrupted time that helped students meet their writing goals, especially dissertation-related writing tasks. Having fellow students sitting nearby, who shared a common purpose, provided a sense of commitment and accountability. The peer support network created through the writing sessions allowed the participants to make progress without feeling isolated and lonely. Students benefited from the sessions to such a degree that they initiated their own versions of the "Write On" initiative. They would meet with group members face-to-face on campus or virtually, through email, at pre-determined times. During the sessions, they would hold one another accountable for setting goals and dedicating time to writing.

According to the author of this study, despite a few limitations experienced throughout (the groups did not attract male participants, for example), facilitating writing groups represented a feasible and inexpensive strategy for supporting doctoral students. According to her,

In a time when many doctoral programs face increased scrutiny coupled with decreased resources, writing groups such as these offer a creative and cost-effective way to enhance both doctoral education processes and outcomes (p. 206).

---

[16] Maher, M. (2013). Write On! Through to the Ph.D.: Using writing groups to facilitate doctoral degree progress. *Studies in Continuing Education, 35* (2), 193-208.

SATURDAY
Week 3 - TIPS & TOOLS

ProWritingAid

Today, if you haven't done it already, spend a few minutes familiarizing yourself with ProWritingAid (www.prowritingaid.com). As advertised on the main page, this tool is not for everyone: Only for "For the Smart Writer". It claims to be "A grammar checker, style editor, and writing mentor in one package".

Whether the claims live up to their loftiness or not, ProWritingAid *is* a powerful online editing tool that allows you to copy and paste your writing project onto their platform and run simultaneous analyses of the quality of your writing. For instance, it will generate a grammar report, a repeated sentence start report (I.e., how many sentences begin with the same words), and even a list of Names you use in the text (useful for catching whether you are over-citing someone's work. Also invaluable is its "consistency" checker, which alerts you to things like spelling someone's name two different ways, or opening a parenthesis and not closing it.

Now, it is important to know the program will not correct the writing *for* you. It will highlight the problems, on the screen, along with suggestions for improvement. Overuse of adverbs is one of my (PG) idiosyncratic patterns, and ProWritingAid makes sure I pay attention to the problem, during editing. The fact it doesn't automatically correct the text is wonderful, because you can learn from each of the changes by deciding whether to accept them, or decline.

Unfortunately, the program does not detect usage problems, if they are grammatically correct. International writers, therefore, if writing for publication in English language journals, will still need feedback from a native speaker.

You can also contact an editor, if you prefer, through ProWritingAid, and ask how much it would cost to have someone (a person) edit the text for you. But using the program allows users to learn something about their writing, while editing. Over time, and with practice, users internalize the corrections they make and improve the quality of their writing.

Give it a try!

SUNDAY
Week 3 - WRITING PROMPTS

Diversity Statement

In recent years in the US, universities and colleges have begun requiring that candidates applying for academic positions submit, along with their Vita and an application letter, a statement regarding their teaching philosophy, research agenda, as well as a diversity statement.

Already during pre-#Blacklivesmatter days, candidates struggled with writing this statement — mainly because they were uncertain of what it should cover. With that movement's and similar ones gaining momentum, the diversity statement has equally increased in value and, some might say, in difficulty.

Dr. Tanya Golash-Boza (Sociology, University of California at Merced)[17] authored a very useful article containing practical suggestions for writing a diversity statement. If you'd like to read the full text, here is the link:

https://www.insidehighered.com/advice/2016/06/10/how-write-effective-diversity-statement-essay

In the article she offers 7 suggestions for authors to consider, when crafting their statement. I list these, below, but would encourage you to read the text for the full development of each suggestion:

1. "Tell your story"
2. "Focus on commonly accepted understandings of diversity and equity"
3. "Avoid false parallels"
4. "Write about specific things you have done to help students from underrepresented backgrounds succeed"
5. "Highlight any programs for underrepresented students you've participated in"
6. "Write about your commitment to working toward achieving equity and enhancing diversity"
7. "Modify your statement based on where you are sending it" [write for your audience].

Today, choose one of the seven points listed above, and set your timer for 10 minutes. Write as fast as possible, non-stop, addressing that point. If your mind wavers and wanders into other points, no problem. After the time is up, set the timer for another 15 minutes and edit/clean up what you wrote.

---

[17] Dr. Tanya Golash-Boza writes the blog "*Get a Life, PhD*", which we highly recommend. Available here: http://getalifephd.blogspot.com/

WEEK 4
Days 22 - 28

"My life has gotten much better since I started writing my own horoscopes!"

MONDAY
Week 4 - BOOKS TO READ

How to Write A Lot [18]

The first of two books Paul Silvia wrote about academic writing, this one is required reading in my (PG's) graduate-level writing course: It deals with the most essential elements of a productive academic writing life in a concise, no-nonsense, to-the-point manner.

By using his own writing and habits as examples, Silvia delivers what he promises in the Preface: a "light-hearted, personal, practical book for a scholarly audience". From a serious look at the excuses academics offer for not writing, through a glance at motivational tools and how to sustain motivation (with "a social support group for fostering constructive writing habits"), to specific strategies for improving the quality of one's writing — the book addresses most of the vital factors academics face in their writing careers. Here's the table of contents, as a teaser:

1. *Introduction*
2. *Specious Barriers to Writing a Lot*
3. *The Care and Feeding of Writing Schedules*
4. *Starting a Writing Group*
5. *A Brief Foray Into Style*
6. *Writing Journal Articles*
7. *Writing Books*
8. *Writing Proposals for Grants and Fellowships*
9. *"The Good Things Still to Be Written*

Silvia's style is, no doubt, light-hearted, personal and practical. What else would you conclude of someone who titles an entire section in Chapter 1, "*Writing is Hard*"? He is a model for scholarly writing, simultaneously engaging and didactic; fun-to-read and sophisticated.

If you never read another book about academic writing, make sure you read Paul Silvia's "How to Write a Lot" (and William Zinsser's "On Writing Well"). In tandem, these books may well be all you need to sustain healthy, vibrant, and elegant academic writing. If you can't read both, however, choose Silvia's. I doubt you will be able to stop there…

---

[18] Silvia, P. (2018). **How to Write a Lot: A Practical Guide to Productive Academic Writing**. 2nd edition. APA LifeTools.

TUESDAY
Week 4 - DEEP PRACTICE

Set Goals for Your Semester/Quarter

If you haven't yet developed the habit of setting goals for your semester/quarter, we recommend you begin. To set these goals, set aside some time (60 – 90 minutes, or make it a mini-retreat sort of time), armed with your to-do list, your calendar, a list of previous accomplishments, your favorite beverage and ambient music (if you like it).

Begin by either developing or reviewing your list of past accomplishments (see page 115, if you never had such a list). Nothing like seeing a list of things you *achieved* last semester/quarter, to put you in a good mood to plan ahead. If, however, you are not satisfied with what you've accomplished, then it is time to reflect and ask yourself why this was the case. Don't forget to account for major events such as a family member's illness, or situations requiring crisis management. These take a substantial amount of time from our schedules and affect our productivity but, often times, we forget about them and think we were merely slacking off.

After reviewing your past accomplishments, list all the BIG due dates for that semester or quarter. Better yet, mind map the semester, drawing the big items first, and then adding all the other smaller items. Reflect on whether what you have mapped is (a) reasonable to accomplish in that time frame and (b) the best use of your time and expertise. Remember: You can always adjust some of these items, by delegating, saying "not now", or simply saying "no".

Determine *when* you need to begin the tasks on your list/map, in order to finish by their deadlines. Then place these items on your calendar or in a "tickler" system (a system containing a folder/holding area for each month of the year; at the start of a new month, you activate that month's folder and address the tasks you assigned yourself).

Don't forget to add to the map of things you *have to accomplish* those items you *would like to accomplish* and are dear to your heart. These may be simple tasks such as, "*Have lunch with a different colleague from the department, every week*", or more complex desires such as, "*I want to see if I can write a grant proposal, this semester/quarter*". Also, add some 'intangible' goals for your work and for yourself – goals that are, indeed, harder to measure, such as: "*Become more patient with students and colleagues*", or "*See my work increasingly cited by other scholars*".

Keep the map or the list of goals. These will guide you in developing monthly goals which, in turn, will help you establish your weekly and daily goals (see page 49 in this book).

WEDNESDAY
Week 4 - HUMOR

"My goal is to be a failure. If I reach my goal, I'll feel successful and if I don't reach my goal, I'll feel successful too!"

THURSDAY
Week 4 - INSPIRATION

If It Works for Others…

What you want is practice, practice, practice. It doesn't matter what we write… so long as we write continually as well as we can. I feel that every time I write a page either of prose or of verse, with real effort, even if it's thrown into the fire the next minute, I am so much further on.

C. S. Lewis

This is the epigraph I (PG) presented at the beginning of my book "Becoming an Academic Writer: 50 Exercises for Paced, Productive, and Powerful Writing". If the notion of *practice* was something C.S. Lewis embraced — if it was good enough for him — it should be good enough for all of us.

If you don't know much about C.S. Lewis' life and career, you may have seen some of his work in movies. He wrote a series of books for children, called *The Chronicles of Narnia*. Disney productions made several of these books into movies, beginning with *The Lion, The Witch and The Wardrobe*.

You may not know, however, what a prolific (and influential) writer C.S. Lewis was (or *Jack*, as his friends called him). A professor of Medieval Literature at Oxford and Cambridge Universities in the 50s, Lewis wrote academic texts on literary criticism. What made him famous, however, were his writings in Christian theology and the Narnia series, even though he also wrote poetry and science fiction.

Today, write a brief paragraph framing *what you believe about practicing your writing*: Do you *really* need it? Has your writing improved, with practice? What can you do to remind yourself, on a regular basis, of the value of practicing your writing? I (PG) often come back to the quote from Lewis at the top of this page, as a reminder.

If practice was good enough for such a brilliant scholar and author as C.S. Lewis, could it be just what we need, as well?

FRIDAY
Week 4 - RESEARCH

A Multicomponent Measure of Writing Motivation [19]

Because motivation plays a substantial role in whether students complete requirements for a college degree, and because college writing requires ample motivation (given the complex demands), MacArthur and colleagues developed and tested a "measure of motivational factors" associated with college writing. They developed the tool for undergraduates, specifically, but you may find it useful for graduate students, also, depending on your context. For example, it may help you identify which of your department's students may need extra support, or how students responded to a writing intervention/program.

To orient readers, MacArthur and colleagues first list the various factors on which they chose to focus, in their study: Factors with an established relationship with "engagement in writing". Those factors include: *Self-efficacy, affect, achievement goals, and beliefs about writing*. In describing and reviewing these factors, the authors do a great job discussing the several theoretical strands and empirical evidence informing our understanding of the writing process (e.g., self-efficacy theory and achievement goal theory).

The study's sample comprised 133 students from a community-college, taking developmental (remedial) writing courses; 50% were men, 49% White and 19% did not speak English at home. Students wrote essays and filled out a questionnaire designed to assess self-efficacy for writing, achievement goal orientation for writing, beliefs about writing, and affect toward writing. Examples of items include: "*I can organize my ideas into a plan that makes sense*"; "*When I'm writing in this class, I'm trying to persuade others with my writing*"; "*Writing helps make my ideas clearer*"; and "*I think that writing is interesting*". Readers can find the items assessing all (scaled) variables in the paper, more precisely, in its Tables.

The researchers found these scales performed well: They generated internally consistent scores and "behaved" in the anticipated ways. The measures, they wrote, "can differentiate between writers of different levels of performance and are sensitive to motivational changes from learning" (p. 39). One unexpected finding, however, was that self-efficacy did not correlate with any of the measures of achievement, despite many available research reports documenting associations between self-efficacy and performance. Authors speculate the nature of their sample might be the reason for this absence of correlation.

Authors end the report calling for further research "to evaluate the motivation scales with a larger and more diverse population of college students" (p. 41). They also add these scales can be useful for faculty teaching writing courses, as a way to capture changes in students' motivations.

Perhaps *you* could find these scales useful for your own work or for the groups with whom you work.

---

[19] MacArthur, C.A., Philippakos, Z.A., Graham, S. (2016). A Multicomponent Measure of Writing Motivation With Basic College Writers. *Learning Disability Quarterly, 39*(1), 31-43.

SATURDAY
Week 4 - TIPS & TOOLS

Tracking

Admit it: You're tired of hearing your prolific colleagues say you should keep track of your writing. Well… they are correct: What you track gets your attention, and at times, all you need to do to keep your writing going at a healthy pace is attend to it. No wonder tracking is a recommendation that accompanies almost any attempt at changing a behavior or adopting a new habit: Exercising, dieting, taking medications, sleeping, walking. If tracking were not valuable, several companies wouldn't be making the amount of money they make by selling tracking devices such as the ones you can wear on your wrist, which count the steps you take, the calories you ingest, the hours you sleep, your heart rate, blood pressure, etc., etc., *ad nauseum* (See? We're tired, too!).

So, today, give some thought to either developing a system for tracking your writing, or to assessing and fine-tuning (if needed) the one you already have. At minimum, keep track of how much time you spend writing. Some writers like to count the number of words they generate every day. Others set a goal in terms of words for a project and keep track of how close to 100% completion they are, every time they write (the writing platform/program SCRIVENER helps you do the latter).

Your tracking system can be very simple. Using an Excel spreadsheet, for example, allows you to customize the columns to house the data you want. By using apps or online resources you can become more sophisticated and keep track of your progress in different ways. Because these applications are revised and/or become obsolete very quickly, we won't make specific recommendations here, but if you search for them you will have no trouble finding the one that best suits your needs.

Some writers still prefer to track using a simple notebook and pen; they log in their start time, end time and total time written, or number of pages generated for that writing session or that day. Whether you have an online or paper-and-pencil tool, the principle remains the same: What you track gets done. You focus your attention on what you're tracking and, at times, that's all you need: To pay attention; to attend to your writing.

SUNDAY
Week 4 - WRITING PROMPTS

Expressive Writing

In 2011, Gerardo Ramirez and Sian L. Beilock published an article in SCIENCE, titled *"Writing About Testing Worries Boosts Exam Performance in the Classroom"*[20]. The authors reported on fours studies conducted with college and middle-school students in the US. They hypothesized that "a brief expressive writing assignment [occurring] immediately before taking an important test" could improve students' performance on the tests, significantly.

The studies confirmed that, indeed, expressive writing could reduce test anxiety substantially and improve performance in important ways. The authors, therefore, concluded: "… it is not any writing that benefits performance, but expressing worries about an upcoming high-pressure situation that accounts for enhanced exam scores under pressure." (p. 213).

Today's challenge involves using *expressive writing* (defined as writing about one's deepest feelings/emotions and concerns) to tackle any anxiety you may be experiencing. For this, choose an issue, problem, or area in your life that raises your anxiety levels when you think about it. Set your timer for 15 minutes (the ideal would be to do this, 15 minutes immediately before you actually need to immerse yourself in the issue or face the problem).

Write freely, non-stop and fast, everything that comes to your mind related to how you feel about that issue/problem or situation. The only rule, here, is *not to stop to think or edit* what you're writing. Just write.

You will find this simple strategy can go a long way toward lowering anxiety levels, especially in academic settings. We, for instance, sometimes ask students to do mini-sessions of 3 minutes of free-writing in the classes we teach, either right before beginning the class, or during the class period, when switching topics or needing a break. When we do this, we find students are much more focused after the 3 minutes, because they have been able to express their concerns and/or capture the mental clutter clouding their working memories. Capturing their thinking assures them they will not forget what needs attention after class and allows them a chance to "sweep" their working memories clean, to handle new material and new ideas. Three minutes per class period. That's all it takes. Fifteen minutes before a high stakes job interview, written test, grant submission, or an emotionally taxing conversation.

Give it a try.

---

[20] Ramirez, G., Beilock, S.L. (2011). Writing About Testing Worries Boosts Exam Performance in the Classroom. *Science 331*, 211: Available: https://pubmed.ncbi.nlm.nih.gov/21233387

WEEK 5
Days 29 - 35

MONDAY
Week 5 - BOOKS TO READ

The Writer's Daily Companion: 365 Inspirations and Writing Tips [21]

Amy Peters' book inspired the writing of this book you are now reading! Peters' book is a compilation of one-page notes and tips on various topics, written, primarily, for writers of fiction and non-fiction. By reading and using her text as daily inspiration, the idea of compiling a similarly useful tool for academic writers took root and resulted in the writing of this book (Thanks, Amy!).

The way Peters structured her book inspired us to order this one in a similar manner: Each day of the week focusing on a category or a topic. Peters' weeks are divided like this:

Monday writings focus on "Writers on Writing", summarizing what other writers have shared regarding the writing craft. **Tuesdays** focus on tips and tricks to fuel the reader's "Motivation" for staying the course of the writing journey. **Wednesdays** bring readers a "Writing Class", offering different exercises to sharpen their writing skills and to encourage them to "try… different formats". **Thursdays** home in on "Editing", with one tip a week for mastering the complexities of text editing. **Fridays** have readers learning about the lives of various writers. This section introduces the reader to writers he/she may not yet have considered reading. **Saturdays** present "Books Writers Should Read", exploring several "must haves" on a writer's bookshelf (and we have borrowed her idea, here, trying to provide readers with books related to writing in general and to academic writing, specifically). **Sundays** bring a "Writing Prompt", with ideas for developing one's writing around fifty-two different topics.

Peters' book is a delight to read and to have next to you as you begin your writing sessions. Even though our book is formatted in a similar manner, it focuses mostly on academic writing. I believe, however, that using both Peters' book and this book (maybe alternate between the two?) can provide important support for you as well as for your writing. Perhaps read one entry from one book at the beginning of your writing session (or during your first writing session of the day) and one entry from the other book at the end of your writing session (or when you "close shop" for the day).

Regardless of how or when you read it, you will find in the book extremely helpful suggestions and, in its author, an empathetic, humble, and encouraging author. When writing about mastering grammar, for instance (on Tuesday of Week 2), she states:

Don't let the fact that you have not entirely mastered the rules of the English language stop you from writing. (…) There is a whole cottage industry of books on grammar just waiting to be read, each of which offers sound advice. I know; I had to read all of them to write this book. (…) My advice is to think creatively first, and then worry if you've written it correctly. Chances are that you'll capture your audience with your wit and prose, and the style [correct grammar] will follow (p. 11).

Bits like this one may well be "just enough" of a spark to ignite your motivation for the writing tasks ahead. And all writers know how precious it is to have live, ignited, always-burning motivation.

---

[21] Peters, Amy. (2012). **The Writer's Daily Companion — 365 Inspirations and Writing Tips**. Fall River Press.

TUESDAY
Week 5 - DEEP PRACTICE

Set Monthly, Weekly, and Daily Goals

If you have established goals for the semester/quarter, this practice will be easier. If you haven't, you can still set monthly goals, regardless.

During my once-a-month planning day — I (PG) do set aside at least half-a-day at the end of each month, to plan for the next month; I mark that on my calendar/planner — I will examine the goals I had set for that semester/quarter and choose a few goals for that particular month. First, I look for everything that has a deadline during month. Those are the first items I list: My goal is to turn things in before the deadline, if at all possible. To do this, I usually place the deadline on my calendar a week or at least a few days prior to the deadline someone else assigned to me.

I also examine the goals I had set for the previous month and take a closer look at the goals I wasn't able to achieve. For these, I will need to decide whether they carry over into this new month, or if I merely need to delete them from my list.

After these, if I am working on projects that don't have an established deadline, I will create landmark goals for them. For example, I may identify: "Finish editing paper on … and begin getting feedback from colleagues/writing group". No strict deadlines here, but a goal to aim for, during this month.

Be realistic, when setting these monthly goals. Remember, months have a fixed number of days, so having 40 large goals to achieve may not be reasonable. Here, less is more. Aim for 5 to 8 "big-*ish*" goals, only. I also like to think about what I want to have listed on my "accomplishments" list, which I will update later in the year. Thinking about items I want to have on *that* list, helps me define my goals for the 4 weeks ahead, a bit more easily.

After you establish your monthly goals list, refer to it when setting your weekly goals. Once a week establish your weekly goals. Many people like to set aside time on Sunday evenings or on Monday mornings, to plan for the week ahead. Whenever you plan your week, make it a habit to check, first, the goals or tasks you listed for that month, still needing your attention. Ask yourself: *"To achieve these things this month, what do I have to do this coming week?"* List those items – choose realistically, again. Your week only has 7 days of 24 hours.

Then, each day of that new week, plan your goals for that day, specifically, but always referring to your goals/tasks listed for that week. Also set a goal for the specific writing project you'll be working on today.

To recall how to set your goals/prioritize for the day, go back and re-read the Saturday entry for Week 1 (page 21) in this book; for how to set a goal for your writing session, check back the Tuesday entry for Week 3 (page 33).

WEDNESDAY

Week 5 - HUMOR

Dear Editor-in-Chief

Here we are submitting our manuscript to be carefully considered (we hope!) for publication in your prestigious journal.

Before taking any action, or even downloading our attachment, would you be so kind to allow us a heart-to-heart moment, here?

Please take a minute and go back thirty-nine years ago when you were young and started your academic career. Remember that first rejection letter you received from a top-notch journal? Didn't it just break your heart? Honestly... didn't it just flood you with negative thoughts about your lack of talent for academia? It *hurt deeply,* didn't it?

How would you have felt, however, had that letter been an acceptance one, or even a R&R? Imagine the possibilities!!! Who knows? You might have been offered the editorship of this journal two decades ago, even! Doesn't this mere thought make you wish you could go back and change the past?

Well... guess what?! You CAN!!! You can make all those good things that did not happen *to you* happen *to us* just by accepting our paper. Yes! You can!

Before you accept our paper, however, we need to make it clear: We are ethical scholars, who would never consciously incur in any ethical misconduct, nor lead anyone else into an unethical scenario. We *do need* your help, nonetheless. Our paper is bad, but it is not *that bad.* With your expertise, experiences, and writing skills, it would only take a little bit of time to anticipate what the reviewers will want to see in the paper, make those changes for us, and then accept our paper!

Isn't this small effort on your part worth the life-changing experience it can bring to all of us? Think about it: The trauma it will prevent; the opportunity to redeem your own traumatic past; and, who knows? Maybe we'll have a chance to become editors just like you, and be able to pay it forward someday, doing the same for other ethical scholars in need?

How's *that* for an editorial legacy?!?

If you would like to discuss this idea further or wish to identify ways in which we can help (but we really don't have time to work on any revisions at the moment — just for the sake of transparency) please feel free to contact us at the address(es) below.

In the meantime, eager to receive your acceptance letter, we remain

Expectantly yours,

Ethical Academic Authors

THURSDAY
Week 5 - INSPIRATION

Working Well

I (PG) was flipping through an old journal the other day — one of those journals that have small prompts to guide the entries you make. I stopped at a page where I had listed all the behaviors I had been performing that were working really well for me, alongside a list of those that were not working very well.

I couldn't believe how encouraged I felt when reading that list of practices that were, at least at that time, going really well! Some, I had abandoned — such as cooking essential food for a whole month, once a month, and freezing daily portions. Some, I maintain still (writing regularly, for example). But in seeing that list, I became motivated to revisit those practices that had worked well, to see if there were any I could 'resurrect' and apply currently.

So, today, we encourage you to begin developing a list (doesn't have to be long at all – maybe 3 items) that are currently working very well for you this semester, and 3 practices that are not working as well. Date those and mark your planner to revisit this list a month from now. In between, you will be thinking about those items and, hopefully, be motivated to invest into more of what's working well and transforming what is not.

Preferably, try to focus the list on elements related to your academic writing. For instance: *Working Well*: Adding 1 minute a day to my writing sessions, so I can get to 45 minutes of writing in each session. *Not Working Well*: Logging how many new words I've generated each writing session.

You will be amazed how an investment of this sort, requiring only a small amount of time and very little energy, can lead to multiple benefits: You slow down and pay attention to your writing; you reflect and pay attention to yourself as a writer; you help sediment your identity as a writer, and you become motivated to keep on keeping on…

FRIDAY
Week 5 - RESEARCH

The Neuroscience of Creative Writing [22]

According to this study's authors: "Previous neuroscientific research on creative writing is sparse and thus little is known about its neural correlates." (p. 1089) They affirm there is some knowledge available on the "motor processes associated with writing", but the "neural correlates of cognitive processes during writing are still unexplored" (p. 1089). Their study, therefore, was designed to provide initial insights into these neural-cognitive processes activated during creative writing. Notice the emphasis, here, remains creative writing – but certainly the lessons learned in this domain can transfer, at least in part, into academic writing.

What they did: They recruited 14 men and 14 women, all of them "native German speakers" aged 24 on average, and "inexperienced in creative writing". Researchers designed a desk coupled with double mirrors so participants could write with their right hand, while lying inside the scanner. A very useful photograph of how a participant's arm and hand were positioned for writing is available in the manuscript (thank you, authors!). Participants would read the description of a task and perform that task before instructions for the next task would be presented to them by a researcher, who remained in the room with participants. The first two tasks consisted of reading a portion of a text and then copying that text, verbatim, for 60 seconds. This copying task served as the control measure. The third task comprised reading the first 30 words presented in task #2, and brainstorming a continuation for that text, without writing. The final task consisted of writing the remainder of the story, brainstormed previously, for 140 seconds.

What they measured: Alongside the scanned data, researchers also assessed participants' creativity with a verbal creativity test (measured outside the scanner). What they found (in brief summary): As expected, creative writing activated additional areas in the brain when compared to copying only, especially areas associated with working memory. Authors acknowledged the creative writing task as one that exhibits a "high working memory load" and "required self-critical attitude of the writer", alongside "domain-specific knowledge … required for creative emergence" (p. 1097). What they concluded: "Taken together, 'creative writing' involves various cognitive brain processes and brain areas representing verbal creativity. Nevertheless, individual literary creativity does not seem obviously localizable in any single brain area or assignable to any single cerebral function" (p. 1098).

What we still don't know: Because this study was the first one of its kind at the time, the authors concluded: "… future research will be necessary to understand the neuronal secret of writing excellent and absorbing literature". Can we make a similar claim for academic writing? Is what makes academic writing excellent and absorbing remaining, still, a secret?

---

[22] Shah, C., Erhard, K., Ortheil, H-J., Kaza, E., Kessler, C., Lotze, M. (2013). Neural Correlates of Creative Writing: An fMRI Study. *Human Brain Mapping, 34,* 1088-1101.

SATURDAY
Week 5 - TIPS & TOOLS

Sketch Notes

We all need tools that can make it easier to generate and capture ideas we have *for*, or *about*, our writing, teaching, research or other projects. One useful tool for generating and capturing ideas is Sketchnotes[23]. According to Mike Rohde, sketchnotes are rich visual notes created from a mix of handwriting, drawings, hand-drawn typography, shapes, and visual elements like arrows, boxes & lines" (p.2). You can see examples of these notes at http://sketchnotearmy.com/ (there are also other books and resources listed at that site, which might be very useful).

Rohde refers to taking notes of ideas in this format as a more *deliberate* way of taking notes. And, remember, *deliberate or deep practice* is a way of performing a task that requires paying full attention, slowing down, and becoming more aware or attuned to what is happening in the present moment.

You don't need to be an artist at all, to use this form of note-taking. You can capture your ideas with words, by drawing big letters, or adding shaped borders around certain phrases and even using two colors (a pen and a highlighter, for instance). Whatever visual effects you add to your notes, these will help tremendously with your ability to recall the information, because at the moment you captured it, you were intently paying attention; because you added visual stimuli, your ability to retain and later recall that sketch increases substantially.

For Rohde, "To sketchnote, you listen closely to meaningful ideas [yours or others', for instance, in a meeting], consider what they mean, and then create a visual map of them. The goal is to forgo the ~~details~~ and instead listen for **BIG IDEAS** that resonate, converting those ideas into visual notes that include both words and pictures" (p. 13)

You can see my primitive attempt to use visual effects to convey my message, in the sentence above (↑), using only my word processor. You can take sketchnotes either by hand or using the computer, the medium doesn't matter.

Give it a try and see whether this manner of capturing ideas for writing projects (or taking notes in meetings, classes, brainstorming during research team meetings, etc.) can work for you.

---

[23] Rohde, Mike. (2013). **The Sketchnote Handbook: The Illustrated Guide to Visual Note Taking**. Peachpit Press. Available: https://rohdesign.com/handbook

SUNDAY
Week 5 - WRITING PROMPTS

My Favorite

Even if we struggle with academic writing, at times, we all have a project that is/was our favorite one — at least during the time we were working on it.

Today, spend a few minutes (not more than 10, if possible) completing this phrase:

So far, my favorite writing project has been ………, because …..

Remember to write freely: Capture every thought in your mind, as fast as possible, not stopping to edit or even to think (no one has to read this afterwards).

After describing the reasons why that particular writing task was your favorite, examine what you wrote: Were the reasons related to the *outcomes* for that piece (e.g., it was accepted for publication in a high impact journal), or were they related to the *process* of creating the piece (e.g., I went to my favorite coffee shop, after a quick run in the morning, and focused only on that paper)?

What you wrote represents valuable data on yourself as a writer, and can suggest a needed change in perspective: If your writing pleasure is attached solely to the outcomes, you may not be enjoying the process and writing, therefore, may be more of an inconvenience than you care to admit. On the other hand, if your focus is exclusively on the process, you may not be challenging yourself enough to get the products finished and pushed out the door, into reviewers' hands.

Conversely, you may identify practices/actions you took that deserve to be sustained — you loved sharing about your project, daily, with a close colleague, for instance. Or maybe you were just passionate about the topic. Period. You would gladly welcome, therefore, any other opportunities to write about it.

You get the picture: Whatever you wrote speaks volumes about you! Learn from that. Adjust, if necessary; celebrate, always! In an ideal world, ALL projects would be favorites. In our real, broken world, we throw a party and have a ball with the projects that are, indeed, favored by our writing soul! They are gifts, rare gifts. Grace upon grace.

WEEK 6
Days 36 - 42

MONDAY
Week 6 - BOOKS TO READ

Journal Keeping: How to Use Reflective Writing for Learning, Teaching, Professional Insight, and Positive Change [24]

Academics who wish to maintain a healthy and steady productivity would do well to develop the habit of journaling their professional careers. If your next questions after reading this first sentence are "*Why?*" and "*How?*", you'll find answers to both, presented in a convincing manner in this book.

Danelle Stevens' and Joanne Cooper's book has many useful features: Part Two, for instance, instructs readers who teach how to incorporate journaling in classrooms and how to handle the issues of grading, electronic journals, and various techniques for effective journaling. Part Three presents case studies for both "*Teaching with Journals*" and "*Journal Keeping in Professional Life*."

No, we didn't skip Part One. We left it for last because it is one of the most beautiful and pragmatic features of the book. Part One provides the *theoretical foundations* explaining *why* journaling works and why it should be used as a teaching/learning tool. If you adopt the practice, you become well-equipped to defend it from observers who might think journaling is only appropriate for seven-year-old girls in elementary/primary school. While girls and boys can, indeed, benefit from journaling, the way in which the authors ground the practice in adult development theory provides a rationale for journaling at any and every age or stage of one's professional and personal development.

And we would like to add: The most useful feature in this book, believe it or not, is the inside-front-cover. There, you will find a picture of the table of contents (TOC) of one of Stevens' professional journals. And yes, it is *real*. We've seen it. She showed the journal and its TOC to us during a workshop she taught at Texas A&M University. Creating a TOC for one's journal, makes ALL the difference. With it, one can quickly search through multiple journals, over several years, and find notes taken during specific conferences, doodles or thoughts generating ideas for a new article, as well as various types of to-do lists. The TOC allows one to quickly and efficiently access all the information needed, no matter how long ago it was captured. If you prefer to develop your journal electronically, many options are out there — but make sure you have a good search feature. If you cannot easily retrieve what you capture in your journal, it is, for all practical purposes, useless after a few weeks. You will not want to waste time searching.

In summary, this book is a must-read. A must-read and *must-do* type of book.

Give it a try! You may surprise yourself with how useful, fun, and exciting it can be! (Really…).

---

[24] Stevens, D..D., Cooper, J.E. (2009). **Journal Keeping: How to Use Reflective Writing for Learning, Teaching, Professional Insight and Positive Change.** Stylus Publishing.

TUESDAY
Week 6 - DEEP PRACTICE

Slowing Down

In today's hectic and frantic-laced world, being told to slow down is akin to hearing "just relax", immediately before a high-stakes exam. Very ironic, indeed. Yet, the notion of deep or deliberate practice — the kind of practice that distinguishes peak performers from mediocre ones — includes the counter-intuitive idea that slowing down will, eventually, speed you up![25]

I (PG) experienced this paradox even before I knew what deliberate practice was. When I studied piano, I had difficulty playing fast-paced pieces. To tackle this, my teacher coached me into exercising my scales very, very *s-l-o-w-l-y*. Agonizingly slowly. And when attempting to learn a new piece, to also practice each bar, very slowly. Ridiculously slowly.

It worked like a charm! I began to play faster, without stumbling. There was something to the slowing-down-and-paying-attention that imprinted the movements into my hands, helped me develop a 'muscle memory' of sorts, and allowed me to play faster than before!

So, today, we encourage you to slow down in your writing session. At least for a few minutes. Set aside 20 minutes to edit one piece of your writing (limit it to a page or a couple of paragraphs, max) – but do it excruciatingly slowly (and don't do this to generate text; you should generate text as quickly as possible, so you're not tempted to edit-as-you-go).

Consider each word choice; question whether you could find a more accurate word or phrase; think about each punctuation mark: How can you maximize its use and aim for a stronger effect? Draft several different versions of a single sentence. Slowly. Contemplate your changes as if you were looking into a fine piece of art at a gallery. Focus on the details; the spaces between words; the words you did *not* choose to write.

When your time is up, resume your normal pace for that writing session. Maybe get back to the slowing down again tomorrow, in your next session. With time you will notice the quality of your writing improving, even your drafts.

But don't take our word for it…

---

[25] Sterner, T.M. (2012). **The Practicing Mind: Developing Focus and Discipline in Your Life**. New World Library.
If you are not familiar with the notion of deep or deliberate practice applied to academic writing, check out my (PG) book, "**Becoming an Academic Writer: 50 Exercises for Paced, Productive, and Powerful Writing – 2nd edition**" published by SAGE Publications in 2016. For a detailed explanation (with examples), see Coyle, D. (2010). **The Talent Code: Greatness Isn't Born. It's Grown. Here's How. 2nd edition.** Arrow Books Ltd.

WEDNESDAY

Week 6 - HUMOR

Dear Google Scholar

Thank you for being so kind: Compared to *Web of Science, ResearchGate,* or any other sources, you have always shown a higher number of citations of my work. I don't really care when others say your numbers are inflated; I call them *generous* and *well-intended,* thank you very much. I am even willing to forgive you for giving my students — who are trying to binge-write their essays a couple of hours before the deadline — access to all sorts of odd and even not-so-scholarly sources. The students may not like what I have to say about their cited sources, but that is *their* problem, not yours.

I realize very little can be done to improve upon your invaluable contribution to the academic communities, globally, but would you allow me this small audacity? I have a suggestion that may, potentially, improve your image among scholars. You know how, every time we carry out a search on your platform, you typically organize the search results with the articles having the highest number of citations appearing first? Has it ever occurred to you that those scholars whose works appears first are already well-established and do not need your support in promoting their work?

Like, what's up with the new Google Scholar Metrics, created in 2020? It lists the "top 100 publications in several languages"…! Who needs *that* as further torture, reminding them they are lucky if their work is even *read* by 10 people!!!

Wouldn't you be promoting a broader knowledge-base if you hid some of the work that is most often cited and, instead, highlighted the publications from researchers who haven't yet been cited extensively? After all, it does take a long time to be referenced by numerous scholars and, as you well know, junior academics like me have only a few short years to establish their impact.

I am well aware of the risks in adopting this strategy. Therefore, in the best interest of the scholarly community, I volunteer as your first pilot participant. I will be happy to send you a list of all the authors whose profiles deserve to be hidden (their citation numbers are obscene!!!). Feel free to delete those and promote my publications instead. I have no concerns; risks are minimal and don't exceed those of letting things remain as they are (at least for me).

Thank you for your attention to this request, and for all you do to support the academic community.

With sincere indexed wishes for your continued success, I remain forevermore yours,

Indexed Academic

THURSDAY
Week 6 - INSPIRATION

Writing and Loneliness — Ours and Yours

One of my (P.G.) favorite quotes from C.S. Lewis is this one:

"We read to know we're not alone."

You can now get this quote on frame wall-art, mugs, and T-shirts, if you'd like… I would just recommend referring to it, once in a while – maybe by returning to this book entry!

The quote brings to life an important truth: Reading connects us with others who either validate our own experiences or challenge them in ways that, sometimes, are life transforming. Written text, especially books, can become true companions and, particularly for introverts, they gain the status of faithful friends.

But if we read to know we're not alone, then the writers of those texts wrote to let us know we're not alone, right? So…They wrote to keep us company. To fill our voids, take up the empty spaces in our hearts and minds. They may not have been aware they were doing so, but they did…

So, here's a mini-challenge for today: As you write, think about the ways in which your writing might be a welcome companion to someone; how your words and the narratives you craft can inspire, enlighten or validate someone else's questions or thoughts. How your ideas, hypotheses, and unveiling of truth can bring hope and promote justice for those whose voices are not often heard.

Today, ponder the question: How is your writing communicating to readers *they are not alone?*[26]

---

[26] We realize some readers may be thinking: "*But I write about technical matters, science, theory…! Not personal experiences, human nature, drama…*". While the argument appears valid, we would counter-argue that even technical writing, as it communicates shared meanings, can provide a sense of companionship to readers who identify with it. Have you never been excited about a technical journal article that happened to be precisely what you were looking for at that moment, while everyone else around you rolled their eyes at it? We have difficulty believing, therefore, that technical/scientific writing cannot fulfill this expectation of communion/companionship. Try another argument…

FRIDAY
Week 6 - RESEARCH

It's Always a Pleasure: Exploring Productivity and Pleasure in a Writing Group for Early Career Academics [27]

Academics world-wide face the pressure to be productive, especially in the earlier stages of their careers. A group of Australian scholars has argued that the "publish or perish" pressure felt by early career academics (ECA) takes away the pleasure of writing from their scholarly practices, entirely. These scholars, based on their experience, proposed writing groups held by and designed for ECAs as a *way to restore pleasure* in writing.

Dwyer et al.'s (2012) writing group is ongoing and comprises five participants who meet regularly, for no more than 2 hours each time. Members submit a writing piece every ten weeks for the group to discuss during meetings. When the group comes together, they discuss the submitted piece which often leads to an " 'Aha!' moment that comes from something discussed" (p. 139). The group members not only provide feedback on writing but also share successes or failures and comment on frustrations of the last ten weeks.

All group members acknowledged increases in writing productivity (i.e. quality and quantity of outputs). Also, the peer support mechanisms facilitated group members' identity development as writers and researchers, helped them with career planning, and assisted with everyday frustrations related to being new to a faculty role (such as time allocation and teaching preparation).

Most importantly, group participants rediscovered the pleasure they lost, related to writing! The writing group functioned as a safe space for members, away from pressures and stressors, to focus on writing and approach it as a pleasurable activity, once again. The following quote from one group member captures the essence of this article:

"I am motivated to write because I need to (...) achieve promotion, but environmental pressures often mean that writing for me becomes functional and instrumental. I must do it, but the pleasure in the performance of writing isn't always there. The writing group provides a regular reminder that writing is a pleasure" (Early career academic - Dwyer et al. 2012, p. 139).

Perhaps academic writing has for you, too, become functional and instrumental. Consider creating a safe space for yourself and other writers, in which the main goal is to restore the potentially lost pleasure of, and joy in, writing! It is certainly worth a try!

---

[27] Dwyer, A., Lewis, B., McDonald, F., & Burns, M. (2012). It's Always a Pleasure: Exploring Productivity and Pleasure in a Writing Group for Early Career Academics. *Studies in Continuing Education, 34*(2), 129-144. Available: https://doi.org/10.1080/0158037X.2011.580734

SATURDAY
Week 6 - TIPS & TOOLS

The List

The essence of life? *Relationships*: We are constantly relating with ourselves, other people, and with the physical environment around us. We cannot escape this essential phenomenon, because we were designed for that.

Among our professional relationships, writing papers, grants, books or other materials in collaboration with colleagues can be one of the most rewarding connections we establish in our careers. They can also become the most damaging ones.

So, today, your task is to develop a matrix (i.e., a table with rows and columns), depicting your most recent collaborators. In the column next to their names, have additional columns where you can capture important characteristics such as: Inside/outside your field; provides best feedback of ____ kind (e.g., conceptual, editorial, language use, tone); reliability on a scale of 1-10 (10= extremely reliable).

Examine your list: Do you need to seek out additional or different collaborators? Or, perhaps, you have become so comfortable with your team of writers, you might risk falling into a "confirmation bias" problem?

As you go through your list, also think how people would depict you and your contributions, if they were undergoing the same reflection/exercise, looking at your name on their list. What strengths do you bring to a collaboration? What could you improve upon? How can your contribution be even richer?

After developing your list, plan to send a thank you note to each of your collaborators for the contributions they make to your academic career and learning. This small gesture can have large repercussions and brighten both your day and theirs!

SUNDAY
Week 6 - WRITING PROMPTS

Reflecting on Feedback

Today's writing prompt consists of filling in the blanks in the items below, during 5 minutes (set your timer), as you write non-stop. The only rule? Do not stop to think or edit. No one will read this, and you may throw it away afterwards.

When people provide feedback on my writing, the most common comment they make is this: " Your writing…
_____

I believe they say this because
_____
_____

There is some (or there isn't any) truth to what they say, because
_____
_____

After capturing your thoughts, examine them closely: Look for patterns (repeated ideas) and issues you can begin addressing. If appropriate, start being more intentional regarding the feedback process, this week. If you wish to read more about a method for feedback giving-and-getting that can yield useful feedback, check out Chapter 5 (*Get Feedback*) in Goodson's book, "*Becoming an Academic Writer*"[28].

---

[28] Goodson, P. (2016). **Becoming an Academic Writer: 50 Exercises for Paced, Productive, and Powerful Writing** – 2nd edition. SAGE Publications.

WEEK 7
Days 43 - 49

MONDAY
Week 7 - BOOKS TO READ

Writing to Learn: How to Write — And Think — Clearly About Any Subject at All

William Zinsser wrote this gem-of-a-book. We know Zinsser a bit better because of his "other" book: On Writing Well. Its 30th edition came out in 2006 and, before that, the book sold over a million copies in an era when advertising was minimal and the Internet, non-existent!

In Writing to Learn, Zinsser claims one can use writing to learn anything. In his words: "Writing is how we think our way into a subject and make it our own. Writing enables us to find out what we know — and what we don't know — about what we're trying to learn" (p. 16).

How to use writing to learn? Zinsser proposes: "The way to begin is with imitation" (p. 14). For him, writers and any other artists or skilled craftsmen/people learn, mostly, by imitating other masters in the field. Eventually, the apprentices move away from the models provided by the masters and develop their own style and ways of crafting. "But nobody", says Zinsser, "will write well unless he gets into his ear and into his metabolism a sense of how the language works and what it can be made to do." (p. 18). In his case, Zinsser learned to write "mainly by reading writers who were doing the kind of writing I wanted to do and by trying to figure out how they did it" (p. 15).

Another fundamental premise underlying the book, is that "writing is rewriting". No way around it. Writing clearly and communicating economically — Zinsser was an avid proponent of eliminating all useless words — are tasks that take enormous effort and should always be viewed as evolving.

Zinsser intended the book to be a compilation of good writing in various disciplines (chemistry, physics, geology and math), but found himself adding quite a bit about his own experience of learning all sorts of things, through his work as a writer and editor. Therefore, the book divides itself rather naturally between these two discourses: Zinsser's own experiences and other writers' in various disciplines whom Zinsser admires.

In summary, if you wish to explore how to make writing more than merely a reporting tool or a self-dictating strategy, and want to turn it into the most useful tool for deepening your scholarship, read the book. After reading, we would venture to say you will most likely agree with Zinsser when he concludes: "…the writing of the book proved one of its central points: That we write to find out what we know and what we want to say." I (PG) thought of how often as a writer I had made clear to myself some subject I had previously known nothing about by just putting one sentence after another—by reasoning my way in sequential steps to its meaning. I thought of how often the act of writing even the simplest document—a letter, for instance—had clarified my half-formed ideas. "Writing and thinking and learning were the same process" (pp viii-ix – emphasis ours).

TUESDAY
Week 7 - DEEP PRACTICE

Capturing Negative Thoughts

In the book she wrote for the lay public, titled **Switch on Your Brain: The Key to Peak Happiness, Thinking, and Health**[29], Dr. Caroline Leaf states:

"Research dating back to the 1970's shows that being introspectively aware of our thoughts in a disciplined way rather than letting them chaotically run rampant can bring about impressive changes in how we feel and think" (p. 76 of Kindle version).

Caroline Leaf is a scientist and therapist who has observed in her own practice and research the effects that awareness of our thoughts can bring about.

So, the challenge for today is this: Observe and capture your negative thoughts. This is, of course, an exercise in meta-cognition, but it will give you both data and a process for imposing discipline in your negative thinking. As you go about the day, have something with you that can easily capture your thinking (a recording device, pen and paper, phone, tablet, or other). As a negative thought pops into your mind, record it. Collect it.

At the end of the day, observe the list of negative thoughts you've had throughout. Challenge them. Ask whether they are true or false; whether they are imagined or real (as in the case of fears and concerns). And, to complete the exercise, write a positive replacement statement, for each negative thought. For example: Negative thought # 20: "I'll never be able to finish this project!" Replace with: "If I spend 15 minutes tomorrow planning how better to tackle this project, I may actually finish this before the deadline!"

If you want to learn more about how to gain control over your thinking and how your thoughts (because they are manifestations of energy) can affect matter (e.g., govern hormones in your body, activate proteins, contract muscles), reading the book mentioned above is a good place to start. Other suggested readings include Lynn McTaggart's *"The Intention Experiment"*[30] and *"Words Can Change Your Brain"*[31] by Andrew Newberg, M.D., and Mark Robert Waldman.

---

[29] Leaf, C. (2013). **Switch On Your Brain: The Key to Peak Happiness, Thinking, and Health**. Kindle Edition. Baker Books.

[30] McTaggart, L. (2008). **The Intention Experiment: Using Your Thoughts to Change Your Life and the World.** Atria Books.

[31] Newberg, A., Waldman, M.R. (2013). **Words Can Change Your Brain: 12 Conversation Strategies to Build Trust, Resolve Conflict, and Increase Intimacy.** Avery.

WEDNESDAY

Week 7 - HUMOR

Attending an International Conference?

If your luck runs out the moment you arrive at your destination, here's what can happen:

- Your luggage is lost, and you need to attend the opening ceremony in your jogging outfit.
- Your presentation is scheduled for the last session of the last day of the conference and only four people show up: The other three presenters and the student in charge of logistics.
- You start a conversation with Dr. So-and-So, a big name in your field. You gush about how her theory has completely and totally transformed your academic life. She gently tells you Dr. So-and-So is over there, talking to that group of students.
- The moment a prospective employer becomes interested in your work, you realize you packed your business cards in the main luggage and forgot them there.
- While chatting with a "big name" over coffee in the morning, you're anxious to make a good impression. During the conversation, this person mentions not being able to get a good night's sleep because the people in the room next door kept flushing the toilet all night long. You ask in which hotel he is staying and choose to say very little thereafter.
- The only person sitting at your table in the formal banquet is a textbook marketing agent who cornered you for almost 45 mins earlier that morning.
- Despite this being an international conference, attracting participants from 45 countries, the only international attention your presentation gets is from the participant who came into the meeting room before you started, asking if you knew where Dr. So-and-So would be presenting. He seemed to be from another country.

THURSDAY
Week 7 - INSPIRATION

A Community

"***A Community of Writers***" is the title of one of Peter Elbow's books, co-authored with Pat Belanoff[32]. Today's entry is not about books or their authors, however, but about finding or sustaining our motivation to keep on writing (or to keep on keeping on, as a colleague of ours enjoys saying).

For this purpose — to have our motivation sustained when we feel like tight-rope walkers, trying to balance ourselves on a thin rope while carrying a heavy and long beam in our hands – communities come in handy. They are both the safety net for the eventual falls and the cheering crowd at the other side of the finish line. Without the safety net, well... you can imagine...

Today's challenge regards reflecting on your safety net and cheering squad: How have they been helpful? What could you or they do differently, or better? In what ways has your writing community supported you, provided information and resources, understood your struggles and cheered you onward? Of course, the enormous assumption underlying these questions is this: You *do* have a supportive community of writers.

You do, don't you?

If you do, jot down a list of 3 ways in which the community has supported you; try also to identify which people, specifically, have been the most helpful and why. Maybe write them a brief message and thank them for what they have represented to you during your writing journey.

If you do not have a community (yet), the challenge is to think about how to get one started. All you need to begin is one more person. The size of the community is irrelevant. The support that can emerge from it is what counts.

Try to identify at least one (maybe two) colleagues who would be open to the idea of forming a writing community. Talk to them and decide on how the community will function (you can try different formats, at different times): Accountability only? Accountability and time writing together? Exchanging feedback? There isn't a single, optimal format; each community will be different and will function differently at different times. The same community might need to vary its format and purposes, over time, also, because they change, too.

Here's the principle: Writing is a lonely task, even when you belong to a supportive writing community. Loneliness can become a barrier to productivity, but it doesn't have to. Focus on weaving a small chrysalis or cocoon of sorts and watch for the benefits. Astonishingly beautiful butterflies tend to fly out of these...

---

[32] Elbow, Peter & Belanoff, Pat. (1995). **A Community of Writers: A Workshop Course in Writing.** 2nd edition. McGraw-Hill, Inc.

Preventing Choking

Geraldo Ramirez and Sian L. Beilock[33] report on four studies testing whether writing about one's fears and worries, prior to a high-stakes test, could help improve test-takers' performance. **What did they find?** In their own words, "Simply writing about one's worries before a high-stakes exam can boost test scores." (p. 211). As simple as that.

Study 1 assessed 20 college students taking a math test. All students took a first test that presented new problems (to control for previous experience). Later, students were subjected to a high pressure scenario: They were told (a) they could win money, depending on their "paired" performance and (b) they had been paired with someone who had already improved their scores on the second test, therefore winning depended solely on their own individual performance. Students were then randomly assigned to two groups: The control group spent 10 minutes sitting quietly before their test; the intervention group was instructed to write "as openly as possible about their thoughts and feelings regarding the math problems they were about to perform."

The variable of interest was accuracy. On the first test, both groups performed equally. In the second test, however, they differed substantially: While the group that wrote outperformed the controls as hypothesized (Cohen's d = 2.48), the control group "choked" under pressure and performed *worse*. Controls had a 12% accuracy drop from first to second test, whereas students who wrote before the test showed a significant 5% math accuracy *improvement* in the second test.

Study 2 replicated Study 1 adding another group instructed to write about "an unrelated unemotional event". The results: Both the control and the unrelated writing groups "choked", showing a "significant 7% drop in accuracy from pretest to posttest". The intervention group, however, "showed a significant 4% gain in accuracy from pretest to posttest" (p. 212).

In studies 3 and 4, carried out with high school students (51 and 55 students, respectively), researchers tried to assess whether this writing intervention would be helpful for students with high test anxiety. In these studies, the control group *also wrote*, but received instructions to "think about a topic that would not be covered on the exam" (p. 213). Both groups, then, wrote for 10 minutes before their exams. What they found confirmed the benefits of expressive writing: "The higher students' test anxiety, the lower their final exam score in the control condition (…) but not in the expressive writing condition." (p. 213). Specifically, among students with very high test anxiety scores, "on the final exam, those who expressively wrote outperformed controls by 6% (…) and performed similarly to lower-test-anxious students, regardless of writing condition (…)" (p. 213).

Their conclusion? "The benefits of expressive writing are especially apparent for students who are habitually anxious about taking tests … Moreover, it is not any writing that benefits performance, but expressing worries about an upcoming high-pressure situation that accounts for enhanced exam scores under pressure" (p. 213).

---

[33] Ramirez, G., Beilock, S.L. (2011). Writing About Testing Worries Boosts Exam Performance in the Classroom. *Science 331*, 211. Available: https://pubmed.ncbi.nlm.nih.gov/21233387

SATURDAY
Week 7 - TIPS & TOOLS

Textbook and Academic Authors Association - TAA

Joining a professional group focused exclusively on academic writing can be one of the best investments you make in your career. An organization "For Creators of Academic Intellectual Property", TAA draws its members from all disciplines, and strives to serve their needs related to writing journal articles and books for academic audiences.

TAA holds an annual meeting for its members and, unlike other professional organizations where these meetings are held to share research findings, TAA's meetings are replete with workshops and sessions in which writers share their tips, tools, and success stories.

Aside from the annual meeting, TAA offers workshops throughout the year (free of charge for their members), access to a rich library of previous webinars and seminar sessions, as well as online writing communities, live chats, and a monthly newsletter (full of tips, tools, and interviews with its members).

Academic writers often claim they don't have "that kind of time", to affiliate themselves with anything outside their silos. Yet a deliberate practice approach to academic writing presupposes you are being mindful of your writing, paying attention to it, investing your energy in it. Joining a professional group of writers such as TAA can only support you and add value to your writing practice (and membership fees are very reasonably priced).

Consider, too, inviting a group of writers at your academic institution, to join TAA and form a local TAA Chapter. Colleges and Universities are taking advantage of what TAA has to offer its chapters, in the form of writing workshops and published resources (e.g., books) for the Chapter's library.

For information on TAA, visit their website: http://TAAonline.net

If you attend one of their meetings, look us up! We might be there, either presenting or re-stocking our toolboxes! Who knows? We even might be attending your presentation!

Enjoy!

SUNDAY
Week 7 - WRITING PROMPTS

Purpose Statement

One of my (PG) colleagues once shared that as a reviewer for a particular journal, he would not continue reading/reviewing a manuscript if he couldn't find – very quickly in the introduction to the paper – the statement "The purpose of this manuscript/report/paper is…". To him, the absence of this statement (or some variation of this wording) signaled a potentially disorganized manuscript. He refused to waste his time.

Having a clear statement of purpose for the writing project you're tackling helps guide not only the reader(s) or reviewers of your text, but serves as a precise roadmap for you, the author. It anchors your writing and prevents you from getting lost in useless tangents.

In the book, Becoming an Academic Writer: 50 Exercises for Paced, Productive, and Powerful Writing, I (PG) recommend that authors spend time carefully crafting a very precise purpose statement. Once worded to your liking, print the statement using LARGE FONT, and post it close to your computer screen or on a wall in your office.

As you write the remainder of the text, always check that purpose statement on the wall and ask whether what you are writing ties directly to that purpose. If not, you may want to flag the text for potential deletion later (but capture your ideas now, as you are writing; don't lose them as they might be useful in another, or in another section of the same manuscript).

Today, then, spend some time crafting a purpose statement for one of your writing projects. Challenge yourself to make it short and pithy: 25 words or less. Begin by generating the statement with no regard for appropriateness, precise wording, or grammar. Then, after capturing your ideas, spend a bit of time editing, cleaning up, and polishing the text. If you can, ask for feedback from someone regarding how "sharp" the statement really is. Print it in large font (size 18 for instance) and place it somewhere easy to see. During your writing session, today, start making it a habit to check what you are writing against that purpose statement.

WEEK 8
Days 50 - 56

MONDAY
Week 8 - BOOKS TO READ

Liberating Scholarly Writing: The Power of Personal Narrative [34]

Robert J. Nash proposes to do a few things in this book that reach beyond the boundaries of writing style or writing technique. He proposes to defend the merit of using SPN — or *scholarly personal narrative* — in academic writing. Nash describes one of the reasons for writing this book, like this:

What I mostly have in mind (…) is to offer you, my readers, an extended reflection on writing, teaching, learning, and living a fulfilled life as a professional and as a person. (…) I will actually encourage you to write about ideas by using the first-person "I" instead of the relying exclusively on the third person "he", "she", "it", or "they". (p. 6).

And Nash's encouragement is grounded in philosophy, epistemology, and effective communication perspectives that have mainly one important goal: Democratize knowledge:

… we have been trained to believe that scholarly writing must be impenetrable to the general public. Any other kind of writing is seen as pandering or, heaven forbid, "journalistic". I, for one, would be proud to be called a "public intellectual." This is someone who, in my mind, dares to bridge the specialized discourses between academicians and the lay public. The public intellectual is a writer who is able to take a complex idea and communicate it in readable English, without compromising its integrity. In the very best sense of the term, SPN writers are "public intellectuals". (p. 8).

Unfortunately, **Liberating Scholarly Writing** is not very easy to find – but we review it here because it was one of the first, in this genre, and would strongly recommend you read it, sometime. Nash has continued developing the notion of SPN in other, more recent books, also. So, if you are interested, below we list two other options, related to Nash's work with SPN.

One cautionary note, however: SPN remains a form of writing and knowledge development that is resisted in certain academic circles. Being aware of this, weigh the pros and cons of using it in your field and your academic environment. Be wise, yet be bold and daring, nonetheless.

His other books:

Nash, Robert J. & Viray, S. (2013). **Our Stories Matter: Liberating the Voices of Marginalized Students Through Scholarly Personal Narrative Writing**. Peter Lang Inc., International Academic Publishers.

Nash, Robert J. & Viray, S. (2014). **How Stories Heal: Writing our Way to Meaning and Wholeness in The Academy**. Peter Lang, Inc., International Academic Publishers.

---

[34] Nash, Robert J. (2004). **Liberating Scholarly Writing: The Power of Personal Narrative**. Teachers College Press.

TUESDAY
Week 8 - DEEP PRACTICE

The Practice Paradox

When it comes to practice, we face an interesting paradox. If one defines practice as Thomas Sterner does in his book The Practicing Mind[35] as "... the repetition of an activity with the purposeful awareness and intention of accomplishing an intended goal" (p. xiv) – then we admit the importance of intentionally setting goals (and we have considered setting goals in previous weeks).

Yet focusing exclusively on the goals themselves, can sap the joy out of practice and turn practice into drudgery. In other words, practice requires goals be intentionally set, but focusing exclusively on goals can make us not want to engage in practicing, thus defeating the purpose of setting the goals in the first place. For complete mastery of a skill, then — in our case, academic writing and publishing — we need to master another skill: The skill of focusing on the process that leads to our goal, instead of focusing exclusively on the goal itself.

Today's challenge, therefore, is this: Reflect on how you've been practicing your academic writing (or any other skill you might be developing alongside your writing). Do the practice sessions bring you satisfaction? Do they add value to your work-life? Do they make you feel empowered and that you are becoming a better writer/scholar? Or, instead, do you face your regular writing sessions feeling dread, anxiety, and an overall sense of futility, because you cannot see any big changes in your writing skills?

The first step in moving toward a more satisfying relationship with your writing practice is to reflect on how tied you are, to your goals of writing and publishing. Do you catch yourself thinking "If only I could publish this paper in this journal, then all will be well!"; "When I get my book published, I will finally feel like I've 'made it'!" If you entertain these thoughts, you are excessively focused on your goals and, it might be safe to say, practice is merely a means to achieve your goals.

Yet, master artisans delight in their work: The painstaking, attention-absorbing, full immersion they experience when creating and refining their work. Most of them will say they enjoy the process more than the outcome (many of us know artists who will just create their works-of-art and stow them away, not even exhibit, sell or give them away; all because they just want the pleasure of making something).

We realize academic writing may not be as pleasurable as creating a work of art, but maybe we could learn something by talking to those writers who delight in their craft (yes, there are many out there!). If nothing else, this attempt to shift our focus (from outcome to process) could bring a sprinkle of happiness to the "daily grind", and just because of that, it might be worth considering, don't you think?

If you feel ready to embark in this focus-shift, start by reading Thomas M. Sterner's book. We reviewed it and recommended, on page 32. Also: Invite a few of your colleagues who seem to enjoy the process of writing/publishing, for a brief chat. Ask them to share the secret of their enjoyment... Prepare to be surprised.

---

[35] Sterner, T.M. (2012). **The Practicing Mind: Developing Focus and Discipline in Your Life.** New World Library.

WEDNESDAY
Week 8 - HUMOR

"I always give 110% to my job —
40% on Monday, 30% on Tuesday, 20% on
Wednesday, 15% on Thursday and 5% on Friday."

THURSDAY
Week 8 - INSPIRATION

Motivation: When You Have None

As common practice, prolific writers do not wait to feel inspired or motivated, to write. They begin writing out of sheer determination, routine, or habit, and motivation usually follows. But what happens when motivation doesn't come? When writing becomes a raw, achy and thorny task of squeezing out ideas, editing what has already been changed at least five times before, of pushing yourself just a bit farther, just one more sentence, one more section, one more paper... and there's no joy, no ease in the movement, your thoughts heavy like lead.

What then?

Sometimes, these moments suggest you might be more tired than you thought, and a break from writing might be exactly what you need. Other times, though, incorporating "writing-for-fun" projects can do wonders! Writing for no one in particular, about nothing special; writing just to have fun with words, to see what silly, or wild, or surprising thoughts emerge – those you never knew you had...

So, for today, if your well has run dry and motivation is becoming more a myth than reality, try one of these:

1. *Write Poetry* – yes, even if you're not a poet. If you don't know what type of poetry, go read a few verses you enjoy, and try to imitate.

2. *Write Haikus* – a form of poetry that has a short stanza, structured either as 5-3-5 (number of words per verse), or as a 5 – 7 – 5 words per verse.

3. *Write complete ideas in six words* or less.

4. *Write a letter* to a friend you haven't seen or talked to in a long while.

5. *Play word games*: Crossword, scrabble, and several other games available online or in print.

6. *Develop a word cloud* from one of your written texts[36].

7. *Start a bullet journal*[37].

Try to make your next writing session be about having fun with the writing, and nothing more. If possible, build in micro-moments of these fun tasks, daily, into your routine for a while. With time, motivation usually finds its way home and starts showing up every day, at your regularly scheduled session. But you'll need to be home...

---

[36] http://www.wordle.net/
[37] https://www.goodhousekeeping.com/life/g30243742/bullet-journal-bujo-ideas/

FRIDAY
Week 8 - RESEARCH

Factors Related to Publication Success

Mindy A. Smith and colleagues (2009)[38] explored reasons why physicians participating in the Michigan State University Primary Care Faculty Development Fellowship Program (between 2000 and 2004) rarely published the manuscripts they had written during their fellowship training. Researchers' main goal was to "explore the role of collegial relationships and institutional characteristics on ever having published and number of publications (p. 121)." Physicians who wish to embark on an academic track are the main participants in these faculty development fellowships.

Of the 90 participants, 87.5% were non-tenure track faculty who spent "an average of 12.7% of their total effort on research and scholarly activities" (p. 121). Their median age was 39 and 51% were women; 75% were Caucasian. About 10% of the fellowship's curriculum addressed the topic of scholarly communications and publication. Other topics included clinical teaching and leadership.

After 4 years, only 11% of the original group had published the manuscript/project they had worked on during the fellowship. Less than half (44%) said they published at least one other paper (not the fellowship project) during that time.

The barriers to publishing were identified as: "lack of time; never finished project/unable to implement/lost data; paper rejected; lack of help; poor quality project precluded publication; lazy/not motivated; left position; not a personal goal to publish; ongoing project; lacked confidence; change in paradigm" (p. 123). The factors facilitating publication were: "home/fellowship mentor; instruction during fellowship; gained confidence; experience of presenting poster; and ' a ton of work and a little luck'" (p. 123). Researchers found significant associations between number of publications and number of mentors and peers "since graduation from the fellowship program", as well as between number of publications and productive local peer support.

The bottom-line findings from this study: a) having mentors and productive peers may represent more support for junior faculty than having collaborators, and b) "aspects of the institutional environment were also found to be modestly correlated with publication success, but no single factor" (p. 125) had a strong association.

Generalizing from the study is not warranted, of course, but these finding can help us reflect on our own and on our colleagues' productivity levels and ask questions such as, "Do I have the support I need from mentors and peers to maintain my writing and publishing productivity?" If you realize you do not have the support, how can you go about seeking it? And what aspects of your institution (department, college, university) are helpful, in terms of your writing and publishing, and which ones are not helpful (or, perhaps, even harmful)?

Take 5 minutes of your writing session, today, and jot down your thoughts as you reflect on these questions.

---

[38] Smith, M.A., Barry, H.C., Williamson, J., Keefe, C.W., Anderson, W.A. (2009). Factors related to publication success among faculty development fellowship graduates. *Family Medicine, 41*(2), 120-5.

SATURDAY
Week 8 - TIPS & TOOLS

Hire an Editor

Academic writing, for some scholars, is so painful and difficult, they view it as a rite-of-passage: Some dark ritual, which they carry out alone, and after much blood, sweat, and tears, bring forth a product that proves they are worthy of membership in the academic community.

These scholars often cringe over the idea of employing the services of a good editor.

Yet, all productive scholars know their writing benefits from different types of feedback at different moments of its development. Certainly, at the final stages, the text profits the most from having someone with a keen eye for details going through the writing with the proverbial comb.

But even the scholars who strongly believe this notion of "useful feedback" sometime feel uncomfortable hiring an editor to clean up a manuscript. They would rather ask a colleague or a co-author to function as the final editor, than to hire the services of professional editors, whose jobs center around making a text near-perfect in format, expression, and clarity.

In an era where many of the popular books are written by ghost writers (a practice viewed as suspicious, by academics), academia is beginning to see the value of having people who are practiced writers help scientists or scholars communicate their scholarship clearly and effectively. Certain fields, for instance, have embraced the notion of seeking specialized help by fully utilizing the services of professional writers and editors. One example is the American Medical Writers' Association (AMWA) — an organization providing writing support services to physicians, in an effort to "promote excellence in medical communication and to provide educational resources in support of that goal"[39]. Association members have graduate degrees in the sciences and are certified as medical writers. They provide support for physicians writing research grants, articles, or books.

Before you cringe and think this is potentially unethical, the organization has a code of ethics that includes, among other principles an attempt to "prevent the perpetuation of incorrect information." Central to the AMWA's mission is the notion of transparency (or acknowledging the help of medical writers in the final products) and of alignment with all other agencies' regulations and ethical codes for writing and publishing in scientific journals.

Even if you're not in the medical field, consider hiring an editor to clean up your text and ensure it is crystal clear. Editors will *not write the paper for you*. They can, however, help your writing shine and communicate your message with ease and beauty. Consider the stakes of the piece you're writing: The higher they are, the more you should think about hiring professional help. And, if possible, hire someone who is patient enough to teach you (or at least *show* you) where your patterns of problems lie, so you may begin proactively addressing them, next time. Eventually, you will become an even better writer than you are right now!

---

[39] https://www.amwa.org - accessed July 25, 2020

SUNDAY
Week 8 - WRITING PROMPTS

Descriptive Writing

In my (PG's) book Becoming an Academic Writer: 50 Exercises for Paced, Productive, and Powerful Writing[40] I discuss how writing the methods section of a research report is perceived as easier (than other sections). The ease comes from this section's focus on describing what the author/researcher has done. In the methods section, the writer has no need to interpret, think abstractly, or make connections to other literature. He/she has merely to describe what he/she did.

Yet, we tend to take for granted how difficult describing can be. Even the notion of what constitutes 'description' is tricky, because it is culturally determined (in general) and, sometimes, field-determined (descriptions of methods vary by discipline and journal requirements). Therefore, many writers struggle with writing clear, precise descriptions.

This prompt will lead you to practice describing. For today, describe the methods used in a study, based on the information provided below. Make up the information as you write but try to keep the description to 2 pages (maximum) or < 700 words.

Here's the information:
1. 100 middle school students surveyed
2. Students – randomly assigned to 2 groups
3. Survey measured 5 variables related to their emotional intelligence and video-game playing
4. One group played a video game for 30 minutes, between surveys. The other group didn't.
5. The 5 variables were measured using standard measures, determined as appropriate for this population, in previous studies
6. Data analysis consisted of comparing survey responses before and after the 30- minute session playing the video game.

As you attempt to describe these bits, ask yourself: "Is there enough detail, here, for an author/researcher who might want to replicate this study?" Then ask: "Is there too much detail, here – or information the reader doesn't really need? (it may be taking your reader on a tangent).

If you find you have a hard time with descriptive writing, try practicing more often. Here's something to try: Pick a photo from any magazine or website. Any photo. Spend 5 minutes, every day, for a couple of days, trying to describe that photo as precisely and accurately as possible. One helpful source, if you feel you need a model of sorts, is the captioning some websites provide to assist visually impaired users learn the information displayed in their photos or graphs. Those descriptions require precision and accuracy. Check it out! With time and practice, you will become quite skilled!

---

[40] Goodson, P. (2016). **Becoming an Academic Writer: 50 Exercises for Paced, Productive, and Powerful Writing** – 2nd edition, SAGE Publications.

WEEK 9
Days 57 - 63

©Glasbergen / glasbergen.com

"You're right, I owe all my success to luck! I'm lucky that my alarm clock rings at 5:00 so I can get to work before everyone else. I'm lucky that my car has a CD player so I can listen to self-improvement programs while I commute. I'm lucky there are electric lights in my office so I can stay late...."

GLASBERGEN

MONDAY
Week 9 - BOOKS TO READ

It Was the Best of Sentences, It Was the Worst of Sentences [41]

The sentence is writing's building block, but in academic writing, we tend to overlook this important unit. June Casagrande's book teaches readers how to craft "killer" sentences.

Most importantly: The book practices what it teaches. It overflows with sentences written with words and structures crafted with precision and beauty. Above all, Casagrande adds a humorous tone to her writing, which makes the pain of learning grammar simply vanish.

The book comprises 21 short chapters, each taking less than 15 minutes to read. Some of the lessons I (MS) have learned, which transformed the quality of my writing included:

- Asking "*What's most important to my reader?*" is all you have to do, sometimes, to structure a balanced sentence.
- Longer sentences can sabotage the writing. Don't try to "cram" information into sentence #1 that could easily fit into sentence #2.
- Listen to your words. Choose them carefully, or you may end up with a sentence that says nothing (or worse – one that communicates the *opposite* of what you intended).
- Choose *specific* words over vague ones. Writing good sentences is about making good word choices.
- Avoid using adverbs. Invigorate your writing by communicating with verbs, instead.
- Know the job of the clauses and phrases in your sentence. Put one in the wrong place, and it modifies the wrong word.
- The passive voice that writing pros consider "bad" is the one that squelches interesting action. Save the passive voice for when you *want* to downplay *who* did what.
- It hurts your writing to use nominalizations in place of actions or descriptions. "I was happy" is far better than "I experienced happiness".
- When you write something in list form, readers expect it to be a list of parallels. Proceed with caution and remember all elements should be in the same form, if possible.
- Omit needless words and clauses that do not really add anything to the sentence (in this sentence, I should have omitted the words: *needless, and, clauses, really, anything*).
- Whenever faced with a problem sentence, look for its main clause. Isolate the main subject and verb. If the subject and verb are troublesome, replace them with the simplest alternatives. Ask yourself what is it that you are trying to say?
- Simplify your sentences with vigorous and action-oriented verbs.

These are only a few examples of the useful tips embedded in this book. These tips, coupled with a witty style and plenty of encouragement will, most likely, make you do a double-take on the sentences you write. Just be prepared: You might be tempted to have a bit of fun with your writing

---

[41] Casagrande, June. (2010). **It Was the Best of Sentences, It Was the Worst of Sentences**. Ten Speed Press Berkeley.

TUESDAY
Week 9 - DEEP PRACTICE

Practicing DOC

In his book, ***The Practicing Mind***[42], Thomas Sterner proposes a strategy (alongside meditation) which, if practiced regularly, can lead a person to emotional stability when facing the rollercoasters of daily life. *Equanimity* is the label Sterner gives to this stability. To reach this equilibrium in the way you react to daily events (those that can make your mood swing from elated to crushed) one needs to practice DOC: *D*o, *O*bserve, *C*orrect (Sterner 2012, p. 114). Seems simple: We're merely need to engage in a task, observe ourselves as we engage, and correct what's needed.

Yet, in order to practice DOC effectively, one of the skills we must master is that of *not judging*. To judge ourselves (and others), we've had a lifetime of practice. It takes practice, also, *not to judge* our actions, especially when it comes to writing. Many of our writing sessions go like this: "I can't move ahead on this discussion section; I'm just no good at this, and I'm horrible at meeting deadlines!" Sterner contends that we WASTE absurd amounts of precious energy when we engage in judgements, and they are wasted because they contribute zero to advancing our goals.

Remember: *Judging* is a behavior, an action. So, for today, practice DOC related to your judgements of yourself as a writer. Observe yourself, all throughout your writing sessions today, and note where your evaluation of yourself needs adjusting. The attempt, here, is to remove negative emotions from the process. As you evaluate yourself (without judgment of good or bad, wonderful or horrific), point to the judgements you have been wasting your energy in producing, and correct them. Instead of "I'm horrible at meeting deadlines", try shifting the focus to a more neutral position: "There seems to be a pattern here: I tend not to meet deadlines. What could I do to break or change this pattern?"

Sterner reminds us that all of this takes deliberate practice, patience, and rest. It can be very tiring to replace old habits with new ones, especially cognitive/mental habits. And, in case you already engage in DOC and in separating yourself from negative emotions surrounding your writing, identify anything that needs correcting in your approach to writing or, better yet, coach someone else into this shift in thinking. Pay it forward!

---

[42] Sterner, T.M. (2012). **The Practicing Mind: Developing Focus and Discipline in Your Life.** New World Library.

WEDNESDAY
Week 9 - HUMOR

Letter from A Journal Reviewer

Dear Author,

I am about to submit my review of your scholarly paper titled "*Examining the investigation of how impact affects influence*", to the journal's chief editor. Most likely, within the next few days, the editor will merge mine with at least one other review, will add a bit of her own thoughts to it and will send you a rejection or a revise and re-submit letter (wishing, deep down, she doesn't have to deal with your paper any longer). Do not worry.

But before all that, I am writing to thank you: Thank you for opening the eyes of this "blind" reviewer, to such beauty and joy! Reviewing your paper brought on a much needed "Aha!" moment. I realized how foolish were my ways...!

Throughout the thirty-plus years of my academic life, like you, I have been submitting papers to different journals. The process invariably comprised: Looking for the right journal, checking all the nitty-gritty details in the "Guidelines for Authors" section, spending more hours than I cared to count fixing the format of both the paper and the references, trembling when emailing the editor a copy of the abstract to see if the manuscript was a good fit for the journal, making sure I had checked at least ten similar papers from that journal, citing a few of that journal's articles no matter how irrelevant they might be, and then submitting the manuscript.

I realized, however, the futility of my efforts, when reading your article! As I read your paper — which started with a discussion (no abstract), a method, and a review of the literature sections, lacked a findings section, used two referencing formats, none of which the journal prescribed, had four different font types and sizes, and included forty-seven typos (before I stopped counting) — I thought about the joy you must have felt when sending out this paper: No effort in writing, no wasted hours formatting, no awkward moments getting feedback, no struggle!!! Just putting something together and clicking the submit button. How free, how liberating!

No matter what the result, I NEVER EVER in my career have felt anything quite like what you must experience when submitting a manuscript. You and I both receive rejection letters, though I must confess I probably get fewer than you do, but just compare the two experiences... Won't you agree that yours contributes significantly to your well-being, and mine to a heart attack? I sincerely wish I had learned this lesson years ago (but never too late, right?).

Don't worry about this paper. It will find its way into a journal. If not this one, maybe in one of thousands begging for content; if not this year, for sure within the next decade. But who cares, right? I am certain none of these matters will bother you in the least. So, once again, thank you for the valuable lesson you taught me, even if it took realizing how foolish I have been.

Wishing you much success in publishing your work,

Reviewer 2

THURSDAY
Week 9 - INSPIRATION

Writing Shoes

The other day I (PG) was walking down the hallway next to my office and saw one of my students walking ahead of me. She wore bedroom slippers. The kind that are lined with fluffy material, nice and warm; cozy and comfortable; definitely *not* dress-up-for-work shoes. And it was not what she was wearing just an hour ago when I had talked to her about some technical matter.

I did a double-take, of course, and couldn't help but blurt out the obvious question, "Slippers?" with a tone that said "You? Wearing bedroom slippers at the office? In plain view!?!".

"My writing shoes!", she said, beaming! "I wear them during my writing sessions at the office, to remind me that I'm in my writing space and it's time to focus exclusively on the writing." And added: "Can't write without 'em!" (she had just left her office for a few seconds to pick up something being printed at the copier). I should also add: This is someone who, despite sharing an office with 3 other graduate students, manages to write productively and ward off interruptions by placing a sign on her door stating "I'm writing. Please come back some other time."

I couldn't help but laugh out loud and think: "Note-to-self – consider writing shoes!"

And, of course, I wondered what other writers might be doing to help themselves, in creative, comfortable, and gentle ways, enter and remain in their "writing space". Academic writing can be so dry and boring, at times, we do need to surround ourselves with ways to gently prod us along, knowing the steady pace will, indeed, reach the finish line.

So, today's question to ponder is quite simple: "*Where are your writing shoes?*"

Increasing Writing Self-Efficacy of Adult Learners

Plakhotnik and Rocco[43] report on improvements made to a writing support service for in-service teachers attending a Hispanic-serving college of education in the southeastern US. The service, Writing Support Circles (WSCs) functions as a "community of learners who work together on improving their academic writing with the guidance of a facilitator" (p. 161). A federal grant helped develop the services and, thus, required regular attendance at the WSCs. Although the 22 participating students (divided into two cohorts) varied in age, teaching experience and marital status, "they were all Hispanic/Latino". Time spent in the WSCs ranged from 4.5 to 6.0 hours, total.

The WSCs' meetings for the first cohort "consisted of a 5-min mini lesson presented by the facilitator followed by reading and critiquing writing samples or student work completed for their classes. The facilitator led the WSC discussion and provided guidance with peer review" (p. 163). The WSCs for the second cohort of students varied from meeting-to-meeting: "the facilitator provided direct instruction to the students, which usually included power point presentations, activities, and answering student questions and addressing concerns." (p. 163).

To evaluate the effects of these WSCs on students' confidence with academic writing, participants filled out a "Writing Self-Efficacy Survey" (adapted from Zimmerman and Bandura's 1994 instrument[44]) and a "WSC Evaluation Survey". Findings from these surveys at post-test showed an increase in self-efficacy ranging from 3% (cohort 1) to 7.5% (cohort 2). The analyses did not control for other factors that might have caused a change, aside from the WSCs.

In the discussion, the authors admit one of the most important lessons they learned from this project was the need to adapt the notion of writing circles, as proposed by Vopat (2009)[45], to account for the harsh reality that students in college and graduate school are concerned mostly about their grades and performance. Shifting the focus of the WSCs from developing life-long writing skills to improving the quality of specific writing assignments, was the change that made the WSCs successful.

Authors end their report by questioning the current approach most schools have regarding writing development for college students. The authors defend the value of providing immediate help to students, first, followed, then, by developing their long-term writing self-efficacy.

While we partially agree with Plakhotnik and Rocco, as we see it, improvements in students' self-efficacy for writing – if done appropriately – can have lasting and transferable effects. So, the challenge remains: To develop learning communities that foster both immediate support (for class assignments), and life-long sustainable writing self-efficacy.

Your thoughts? What approach and services does your school/university provide to support students' academic writing? How about support for faculty's writing? Start questioning.

---

[43] Plakhotnik, M.S., Rocco, T.S. (2016). Increasing Writing Self-Efficacy of Adult Learners: Difference Approaches, Different Results. *Adult Learning, 27*(4), 160 – 167.
[44] Zimmerman, B.J. & Bandura, A. (1994). Impact of self-regulatory influences on writing course attainment. *American Educational Research Journal, 31,* 645-862.
[45] Vopat, J. (2009). **Writing circles: Kids revolutionize workshop**. Heinemann.

SATURDAY
Week 9 - TIPS & TOOLS

Daily Steps

Not making as much progress on your writing as you would like to?

Try this: Every day, during your first writing session, or during the time you use to establish your goals for the day, list 3 small action steps you will take, today, to advance your writing.

These action steps should be worded as dynamic verbs, such as: List, map, write, define, call, check, ask, invite, analyze, summarize, compile, sketch, edit, clean up, sort, organize, delete, reduce, add, follow. They should represent concrete actions you will take, related to the writing you want to advance, today. Avoid actions that cannot be seen, such as "plan project Z", or "consider using method B". Planning and considering are actions you can mentally engage in. Here, we're looking for actions you need to physically engage in, such as "List 3 -5 steps I need to take in planning for project Z"; "Draft an email to so-and-so, suggesting we consider method B for our study". Listing and drafting engage your senses, your whole body. That's what you should be listing. Finally, the steps should be small and achievable. Make them as small as you can. In doing so, you will lower your resistance to them, and begin. Establishing ridiculously small tasks helps avoid procrastination and gets something done. Remember: If you're trying to make your writing "move", doing something is always 100% better than doing nothing.

Tomorrow, establish 3 more steps you will take that day, to advance your writing.

If you stay with the list and perform the tasks, you will see your writing move ahead. Don't forget, however: Each step should be some sort of action or behavior you can accomplish that day. If the steps cannot be accomplished in one day, break them down. For instance: If you still need to perform certain analyses of your data, establish as one step for today: "Run descriptive analyses, today (and let all other analyses fall in tomorrow's category)". Or, if needed, make all three action steps for today center on your analysis: (1) Run analysis X; (2) Run analysis Y; (3) Develop the skeleton for the table reporting analysis X and Y.

The principle, here, is this: You are taking some action, however small, to advance that particular piece. After all, if writing is a succession of good bits and good moments, after a while these small steps will have taken you quite far ahead; much further than you would have gone, otherwise.

SUNDAY
Week 9 - WRITING PROMPTS

Reflections on Writing

Today's writing prompt consists of filling in the blanks in the prompt below, during 3 full minutes (set your timer), as you write non-stop:

When people provide feedback on my writing, the most common comment regarding my writing is this: " Your writing _____

_____ "

I believe the reasons people say this are:

_____

_____

_____

WEEK 10
Days 64 - 70

"My cell phone helps me be a lot more productive. Especially when I turn it off."

MONDAY
Week 10 - BOOKS TO READ

A Guide to Publishing for Academics [46]

Ever wonder what journal editors (especially those that rejected your work, recently) really want? Rarely is it obvious —from the terse desk-rejection notice you received saying your article doesn't fit the aims and scope of that journal. *What are they thinking?*

In the book **A Guide to Publishing for Academics**, you'll find the answer (most likely, in Chapter 6, titled "*How Could My Paper Have Gotten Rejected?*"), authored by James R. Marsden. Other chapters also might help answer your question, as they address scientific publication issues (in journals, mainly), ranging from trying to convince writers that editors really want to help (see Chapter 10, *The Editor is Often a Coach*), to addressing the unique challenges faced by researchers whose native language is not English (see Chapter 14, *Lost in Translation and Other Challenges of New and International Researchers Seeking Publication*). Within that range, you are bound to find very helpful insights and suggestions you can apply to your own work.

Edited by Jay Liebowitz — someone who spent "24 years as the founding editor-in-chief" of a publication called *Expert Systems with Applications: An International Journal* — all chapters' authors are involved in some form of editorial role in various academic journals. Their experience, expertise and perspectives make this a unique and extremely useful book. Here's one example:

Chapter 1, written by John S. Edwards (founding Editor-in-Chief of the *Knowledge Management Research and Practice Journal*), writes about lessons that, especially junior faculty should pay close attention to. Lesson 5, writes Edwards, begins with: "If in doubt, ask the editor". And he adds:

> "As a junior academic, you might think that you shouldn't waste the time of busy senior people with what might be trivial inquiries. Actually, the opposite is true, at least of journals. If your paper does fit most editors will welcome the initial contact as a chance for clarification on both sides. If it does not fit, then you will have saved everyone's time, including the editor's and reviewers' as well as your own" (p. 8).

This is only an example of the many useful tips and suggestions this book makes. In answering the question, "*What are they thinking?*", you may learn a thing or two and even begin to appreciate more the hard work that goes into editing a journal.

Who knows? Some day you may become that editor and will need to be prepared to answer the question, yourself.

Note: Yes, the book is "dated" by now, having been published in 2015. However, most of the insights and suggestions offered there are timeless and, therefore, still quite relevant. You'll see…

---

[46] Liebowitz, Jay (Editor). (2015). **A Guide to Publishing for Academics: Inside the Publish or Perish Phenomenon**. CRC Press, Taylor and Francis Group.

TUESDAY
Week 10 - DEEP PRACTICE

Reading With Purpose

Because deep or deliberate practice entails slowing down in order to concentrate attention on the task we're performing, we should apply the strategy when reading the professional literature that informs our writing. For many academics, mastering the review of the literature represents a daunting task, often assigned to an eager graduate student who is seeking to be initiated in the field.

The most useful way to slow down and really pay attention to what we are reading (especially when reading for a writing project), is to begin by answering the question: "What am I reading this literature for?" Or stated differently: "What is the purpose of my reading this literature?"

To answer this question, try to come up with a very well-defined and delineated purpose. For example, "I am reading this literature to learn how many studies support my hypothesis and how many do not". Or, "I am reading this literature to learn what methods are most commonly used, when studying this particular subject."

Whatever the purpose, make it as concrete as possible. Make it, so if you need to delegate the reading and organizing of the literature to that eager graduate student, you can do so, mid-way through your reading and expect the student will be able to cull the same information that you were collecting from the literature. In other words: The purpose for reading is so clear, you both are calibrated and 'on the same page' when collecting information from each piece/text.

Make the purpose very specific; as specific as you can. It's okay to have two very narrow purposes that relate closely to each other. For instance, read searching for which methods have been used and what references authors cite in support of those methods. Two purposes, but very closely aligned.

Even if you need to re-read the same pile of articles, searching for different bits of information, because you are focused on a narrow purpose you will pay more attention to that particular information. Later, when searching for something else, you will focus – again–exclusively on searching for that information.

As you capture the information you need, consider organizing it onto a Literature Review Matrix[47] format, for easier searching later on.

You will see that you'll be able to retain and recall the information better than if you had just read the literature, broadly, to "familiarize" yourself with the topic, without a defined purpose.

Give it a try, today or when you need to tackle the literature review for your next project(s).

---

[47] To learn how to develop and use a Literature Review Matrix, see: *Appendix A* in: Goodson, P. (2016). **Becoming an Academic Writer: 50 Exercises for Paced, Productive, and Powerful Writing** – 2nd edition. SAGE Publications.

WEDNESDAY
Week 10 - HUMOR

A Writing Carol

Dear Last-Minute Writer,

Do you work better under pressure? Do you believe your mind is "sharper" when meeting a tight deadline? Are you proud of the sleepless all-nighters you pulled to deliver your writing on time?

If you answered "yes" to any (or all) of these questions: STOP IT!

I am the Ghost of your Binge-Writing Past. I saw how many times you re-read your work after submitting it, wanting to bang your head against the wall because you found silly typos you missed. I was the one who witnessed how often you developed a strong argument for your work a couple of days after you rushed to meet the deadline (when you had been desperate for a strong argument while you wrote in a rush). I watched you when you found – a couple of days after submitting -- some extremely relevant literature that could have changed the direction of your work for the better. I was the one who heard all the empty promises you made, not to leave your writing for the last minute, repeated like a mantra to yourself, when your eyes were frog-like from lack of sleep and staring at the monitor.

My question to you: HAVEN'T YOU HAD ENOUGH?!

I know! I know. I sound like one of the ghosts in the Scrooge story about Christmases past, but they did a good job towards the end of the story, didn't they? Just one more question: When you are preparing to go to a job interview, an important meeting, or to a family event, do you make sure you pick and wear the best clothes you have, or do you just ensure you're wearing something? Do you try to show your best self or only an acceptable self, who made it to the event on time? WHY THEN would you submit last-minute work as if leaving home without even looking at the mirror? As if you are OK with wearing anything as long as you are not naked and not late?!?!

OK... this ghost will shut up, for now. I will return before your next deadline, for sure.

Merry Writing!

Ghost of Binge-Writing Past

PS: Don't tell anyone, but I once was a role model for all that last-minute stuff, too. But, then again, I'm a ghost. I don't have to worry about what I wear...

THURSDAY
Week 10 - INSPIRATION

Writing? What's THAT?

What's your definition of writing? Have you ever thought about it? What counts as writing, for you, and what doesn't?

I've (PG) always found the question interesting, especially because I always get questions and comments, when I teach writing productivity, like this: "Can I count reading as part of my writing session?", or "I spent a lot of time developing these test questions for my students, so I didn't do any writing this week".

For many academics, writing is the task that gets done after all the data are collected and analyzed. Their writing only comes in the form of journal articles, research reports, grant proposals or books and book chapters. Nothing else counts as "real writing".

I would challenge this notion. Writing can be (and I would argue should be) viewed more broadly. For me (PG), writing is the task of organizing elements into cohesive and coherent units that create meaning of some type. These elements are symbols, and they can be words, but they also can be numbers (as in writing a mathematical equation/proof), computer code, shapes, images (as in putting a presentation together), and even colors and sounds (as in painting or composing a melody).

If viewed in this broader manner, we discover we write more than we think we do. Viewed this way, writing becomes a way of organizing and making sense of disparate elements. We can, therefore, use writing to organize and make sense of our own thoughts, to express our deepest, most difficult-to-articulate feelings, and even to rehearse difficult conversations with others or solve challenging problems.

So, what is your approach to (or definition of) writing? If merely a dictation tool, so you can communicate your research findings, fine: This is, indeed, one of its many applications. But have you ever tried using writing to learn something new? Have you ever tried writing using other types of symbols, besides words?

Recently, I learned that embroidery samplers (a type of image developed with embroidery stitches, popular in North American culture) were developed to teach certain stitches to other embroiderers, given there were no printed patterns, books, or manuals, way back when (we're talking 18th century or earlier, here). These samplers were, therefore, the textbooks for those wanting to learn embroidery. The samplers were the books; the stitches were the words. Writing with stitches — which, by the way, often included embroidering the whole alphabet and numbers from 0 to 9, alongside entire verses, phrases, or words. Making meaning with fabric and cloth – another form of writing…!

Today, then, take 5 minutes to jot down some thoughts about how you view and define writing and how you have been using this most eclectic and remarkable tool. If you've already discovered the broader benefits of writing, then welcome to the club! If, on the other hand, you haven't yet experienced much that is positive, talk to us (PG, MS, and MB) — or better yet: *Write* to us. We'll be happy to help you change your mind!

FRIDAY
Week 10 - RESEARCH

Writing Anxiety and Writing Self-Efficacy

In this study (authored by two of us – PG and MB – and one other colleague[48]) researchers observed a sample of graduate students at a research-intensive university in the southwestern United States, regarding their writing anxiety, self-efficacy, self-awareness and self-management. Very little research has examined graduate students as academic writers, despite abundant data (published mainly in the 1980s and 1990s) on faculty.

Graduate students in this study participated in POWER Writing Studios. POWER — an acronym for Promoting Outstanding Writing for Excellence in Research — comprises a set of support services available to graduate students at Texas A&M University. The Studios are free of charge, informal, and total 8 hours (2 hs x 4 weeks) of exposure. The sample included 174 students who volunteered to complete an anonymous online survey, before and after their Studio. The data in the report summarized here covers only the pre-test surveys and represent a snapshot in time of what characterizes this group as academic writers.

While study participants were from various disciplines, campus-wide, most were women (60.8%), with an average age of 30 (SD=6.9; range 20-54). Half the sample (55.2%) reported English was not their first language.

Among the most important findings in this study were:

- Writing self-efficacy (or the confidence one has in his/her ability to write effectively in academia) was a strong and significant predictor of writing anxiety, while self-awareness and self-management were not.

- When controlling for self-efficacy (i.e., assuming everyone has the same confidence level), gender remains a significant predictor of writing anxiety (with women reporting higher anxiety).

Some troubling questions arise from these findings, especially regarding women academic writers: Why, for this sample, having strong confidence in one's ability still didn't lower writing anxiety among women writers? We can speculate about several factors (none of which were measured in this study), such as: One may have confidence in one's own ability, but not trust the system to reflect that ability adequately; one may be confident writing papers, books, grants, but still experience anxiety regarding the outcomes (the publications, the awarding of monies); one may be confident in one's ability, but aware that ability may not be enough, when one's work is continually evaluated by peers.

Lessons learned from this study suggest academia should invest in building students' self-efficacy regarding their academic writing, alongside developing support systems to help students cope with their anxiety (one successful example is the POWER Service, mentioned above. For more information, see http://power.tamu.edu).

When it comes to academic writing, skills are not enough. Emotions need addressing, too.

---

[48] Huerta, M. Goodson, P., Beigi, M., Chlup, D. (2016). Graduate students as academic writers: writing anxiety, self-efficacy and emotional intelligence. *Higher Education Research & Development, 36*(4), 716-729. Available: https://doi.org/10.1080/07294360.2016.1238881

SATURDAY
Week 10 - TIPS & TOOLS

Mind Mapping

Many academic writers become stalled when they begin by, first, outlining the project. Outlining is one of the main strategies responsible for "writer's block".

Outlining seems like a great place to start a writing project, because it presupposes the writer begins with some sort of structure and ordered sequence to follow. The order and sequencing function as guidelines for the writing, much like the dark outlines in a coloring book function as a guide to color between the lines. And outlining is, indeed, a great idea, when the writer already has a good sense of how he/she wants to structure or order his/her ideas in that particular writing piece. It is a horrible idea, however, if the writer has no clear sense of how to order the ideas, or even of which ideas will 'survive' in the final piece, and how they will all connect.

Much of the academic writing we do is already outlined for us, in a way. The IMRAD format (Intro, Methods, Results and Discussion) is an a priori outline we follow when writing journal articles. Presentations at conferences are another example. Nonetheless, quite often our writing starts with a very insipid idea and with no or few clues as to how best to order it. In these cases, forcing ourselves to produce an outline before writing the text can be agonizing and counter-productive.

Why? Because when we create/generate text, we are seldom thinking in order/sequence. The creative process is messy, non-linear. We make associations and connections that are, at times, ridiculous or unfeasible. Such is the nature of creativity. At that moment, our attention is not in the details related to order, sequence, flow: All of these come later, during the editing phases of the project.

One tool for generating and capturing ideas, then, without concern for outlining: Mind Mapping. If you Google or look for Mind Mapping on YouTube you will find several videos showing how the technique is used. The essence is this: Develop a network of ideas on a single sheet of paper (or screen), in a manner that allows you to visualize all the ideas simultaneously, to make connections you wouldn't have thought of making, and to capture everything you want to tackle in your writing piece — all in one place.

There are several online tools (some are free[49]) to help you develop electronic Mind Maps that you can share with your co-authors. Consider developing a Mind Map for each of the sections of your writing piece: one for introduction, one for discussion, for instance. The goal is to capture, capture, capture. Make sure you have jotted down all the ideas you believe are important to present. Then, choose one small arm or portion of your Mind Map, and develop a couple of paragraphs about that piece. In the next writing session, choose another small chunk of the map to write about. How the pieces will be ordered, you will decide later. As your chunks develop, you will begin to have a sense of what should be put first, and what comes next.

Give it a try!

---

[49] One free tool is Coggle. Available at: https://coggle.it/

SUNDAY
Week 10 - WRITING PROMPTS

Reasons Why

In academic writing, authors must provide a cogent, logical explanation why they are engaging in that particular research or writing project. The "Rationale", they call it; the reasons why.

Researchers engage in research for various reasons: To address controversies in their fields, to propose innovative methods or theories, and to question a field's main assumptions. The reason provided most frequently, however, is the need address a gap in the existing knowledgebase. Many graduate training programs place considerable emphasis in training students to search for such gaps and make contributions, as tiny as they may be, toward filling them.

When presenting the rationale for these projects, however, oftentimes we see stated as a rationale, only something similar to, "We are doing this, because there is a gap in the current literature, or because nothing like this has been done before".

The "nothing-like-this-has-been-done-before" reason appears very seductive, especially for novice researchers and researchers in training. It appears compelling because it took a huge amount of work and time-on-task to even detect that gap and determine that it was, for all legitimate purposes, a real one!!!

Nonetheless, the absence of literature/research on a given topic or niche does not, necessarily, indicate a vacuum that must be filled. It may be a blank space in the literature because, simply, it cannot be done: Filling that gap would entail unethical behavior, unfeasible logistics, or unrealistic time frames. A literature gap, therefore, does not a relevant topic make. It is perfectly appropriate to mention in a report of the work that this approach or this topic has never been examined or employed before, but this should not constitute the main portion of your rationale.

An appropriate rationale should answer the reader's question: "OK, there's a gap in the literature. Why is filling this gap important?" Or, in simpler terms: "Why should I – the reader, the reviewer, the grant agency – care?"

Today, then, set aside 15 minutes during a writing session to examine how you worded the rationale for one of your projects (if you have more time, take a look at several projects). Do you have a compelling answer to the "Why should the reader care" question? If not, begin to capture your answers in a draft and refine them later.

And, don't forget this important step: After you write, get feedback from a few colleagues on the rationale alone. Ask feedback givers if they believe what you wrote answers the question clearly. If not, keep fine-tuning the statement until it does. And try to learn as much as you can about the audience for your piece. Write to them: Why should they care?

Just in case you're wondering why we believe you should care about what we wrote above, here is our reason: A strong rationale(s) may constitute the difference between readers reading your piece in full, or not; voting to fund your project, or not; supporting your promotion and tenure, or not.

Compelling enough…?

WEEK 11
Days 71 - 77

MONDAY
Week 11 - BOOKS TO READ

The Artist's Way — A Spiritual Path to Higher Creativity [50]

Okay, okay... we used the 'S' word, here, and some of you may have, suddenly, become uncomfortable. What does spirituality have to do with academic writing?

In fact, more than you would think. However, before you turn the page and switch to more 'brainy' topics in the following pages, please allow yourself to consider there might be other dimensions to the visual reality we experience on a daily basis – and consider, too, that these unseen dimensions may represent a generous storage of inspiration, motivation, and creativity? Would you also consider the notion that science (as art) relies heavily on the creative process, the spark of which often emerges from sub-conscious minds, from dreams (the kind of dreams one has when sleeping or day-dreaming), and random connections people make?

If you agree creativity does play a central role in the academic life, and not merely in the lives of visual or musical artists, this book provides useful insights and helpful approaches. The cover declares at the very top: "A Course in Discovering and Recovering Your Creative Self". And so it is. And because it is structured to reflect the workshops Julia Cameron teaches (helping artists, professionals, and people from all walks of life 'unblock' and re-harness their creative energy), there are weekly readings and exercises to practice each week – 12 of them. The most essential tools she will promote: Daily writing (what she calls "Morning Pages") and "Artist Dates" (blocks of time during the week "especially set aside and committed to nurturing your creative consciousness, your inner artist" (p. 18 of 1996 edition).

If you don't think of yourself as an artist, nor of your writing as a particular form of art, you probably don't know that most Nobel Prize winners in a particular study "were significantly more likely to engage in arts and crafts avocations" than other groups of scientists to whom they were compared, and more than the U.S. public in general[51].

If it's good enough for them, could it be good enough for you?

---

[50] Cameron, Julia. (1992; 2016). **The Artist's Way: A Spiritual Path to Higher Creativity**. 25th Anniversary Edition. Jeremy P. Tatcher/Perigee Books.

[51] Root-Bernstein, R., Allen, L., Beach, L., Bhadula, R., Fast, J. Hosey, C., Kremkow, B., Lapp, J., Lonc, Kaitlin; Pawelec, K., Podufaly, A., Russ, C., Tennant, L., Vrtis, E., Weinlander, S. (2008). Arts Foster Scientific Success: Avocations of Nobel, National Academy, Royal Society, and Sigma Xi Members. *Journal of Psychology of Science and Technology*, *1* (2), 51 – 63. p.51)

TUESDAY
Week 11 - DEEP PRACTICE

What Is Your System?

Two of us (PG and MS) enjoy needlework as a hobby. We especially enjoy the very large and intricate projects in cross-stitch. Modern designs for cross-stitching can have the equivalent of ¼ to half a million embroidery stitches in the designs! Imagine drawing a picture one pixel-at-a-time, using 250,000 pixels: That's what these intricate cross-stitch patterns are like. Needless to say: These projects can be daunting, and many people shy away from them given the magnitude of the task.

These projects remain seemingly impossible, however, only until one realizes they CAN be done: All that's needed is a system (and also patience and passion, but we will assume these, for now). A system is a set of elements. A dynamic system is a set of elements that are continually interacting and affecting one another. We would argue that competent academic writing emerges out of a dynamic system of interacting elements. These primary elements are: You (the writer), a set of strategies, a set of tools, and support.

If you think about it: Often when we're stuck in a task, or something is just "not working, one reason might be that we lack a system for tackling the task. For example: Clutter. People who struggle to manage clutter usually lack a set of strategies, tools, and support for managing the "stuff". When they develop a way of handling objects and have a designated place for everything, they know what to do, every time; they have the right tools and people around them to reinforce, validate, or help.

So… what is your system for tackling the daunting academic writing tasks in front of you? What are your strategies? Which tools do you use? Who is part of your support system?

Hopefully, you have well-defined answers for each of these questions. You know what to do and how; you know what resources are available around you, and you have people close by to provide emotional support and feedback.

In case you don't have a functional system yet, consider taking a look at a couple of resources that could help you develop one: The books by Goodson, Silvia, Gray, and Stevens can help[52]. These books are replete with strategies, tools, and ways to obtain useful support from people around you.

Tackling academic writing without having a system will be agonizing and self-defeating (to put it mildly). There's no reason to make it so. Today, then, reflect for a bit on what is your system for writing: If you have one, see if it needs fine-tuning; if you don't have one, start by determining to build one, and seek out these resources. You'll see the difference it can make…

---

[52] Goodson, P. (2016). **Becoming an Academic Writer: 50 Exercises for Paced, Productive, and Powerful Writing** – 2nd edition. SAGE Publications.
Silvia, P. (2018). **How to Write a Lot: A Practical Guide to Productive Academic Writing.** 2nd edition. APA LifeTools.
Gray, T. (2020). **Publish & Flourish: Become a Prolific Scholar.** 15th Anniversary Kindle Edition.
Stevens, D. (2018). **Write More, Publish More, Stress Less! Five key principles for a creative and sustainable scholarly practice.** Stylus Publishing.

WEDNESDAY
Week 11 - HUMOR

Top 10 Tips for Becoming a Terrible Academic Writer

10. Never re-read what you write (you're a perfectly good writer and, of course it's clear!).

9. Never ask for feedback (your work is no one else's business).

8. Write as close to the deadline as possible (you *love* the adrenaline rush).

7. Never read about writing (it's a complete waste of time).

6. Never read other people's work (just distracts you or, worse, makes you jealous).

5. Never share frustrations regarding your academic writing with others (see Tip # 9).

4. Never stick to a plan (developing writing routines only adds to the stress).

3. Repeat this affirmation daily: "You get rejections because you are not good enough."

2. Never join a writing group (someone is bound to steal your ideas or make you feel incompetent).

1. Never collaborate with junior academics (seek out only the big names)

THURSDAY
Week 11 - INSPIRATION

Writing to Slow Down

On every level of life, from housework to heights of prayer,
in all judgment and efforts to get things done,
hurry and impatience are sure marks of the amateur.
Evelyn Underhill

I (PG) read this quote in "One Thousand Gifts: A Dare to Live Fully Right Where You Are" (one of my favorite books[53], by Ann Voskamp). I've read the book several times and each time the quote forces me to take a hard look at, and question, my life "lived amateur", as Ann would say. It forces me to face my harried and hurried attempts to get things done, to be productive, and I wonder…

I wonder whether I have succumbed to the temptation of this era: To value efficiency more than effectiveness, product over process, immediacy instead of immersion, speed before precision. Because "hurry always empties a soul", writes Ann, I wonder if I have lived amateurishly and continually emptying.

As I wonder, however, I remember: I write every day. The routine and daily grind of capturing and weaving words help me slow down; help me pay attention. Indeed, I conclude, it is because I write daily that I live life "less amateur", less hurried, less empty. It is precisely when I slow down to write that I become more efficient.

Paradox: Easier said, than done, of course, because I struggle with the practice. I bet you struggle, too. So, where to begin? Maybe, here:

Sit at your computer and stare at the screen for at least 15 minutes. Don't write anything. Spend the time imagining where you would like the writing to take you.

Check out the International Institute of Not Doing Much (http://slowdownnow.org) for a coherent rationale for slowing down, if the one I presented above does not convince you.

Schedule power naps during the day, or during the week.

Spend some time reading for pleasure. Only reading.

Have conversations about writing, with some of your favorite people.

During a writing session, do not write text. Instead, play with isolated words, without concern for meaning. Play with them because you like how they sound, or how you feel when you write them, or how they look when typed. Play with developing word clouds. Read "Poemcrazy" by Susan G. Wooldrige[54] if you need permission to play.

Fair warning: As you write-to-slow-down, funny little surprises will begin to pop-up. You'll begin to notice people, events, and places you had previously ignored. You may even recover some of the joy in writing, you thought you might have lost… Side effects and hallmarks of a non-amateur life.

---

[53] Voskamp, A. (2011). **One Thousand Gifts: A Dare to Live Fully Right Where You Are**. Zondervan.
[54] Woolrdge, S. (1996). **Poemcrazy**. Three Rivers.

FRIDAY
Week 11 - RESEARCH

Micro-Breaks

It's your writing session and you just got up to get a cup of coffee. After a few more minutes of writing, you check your Instagram account. Your write a couple of pages and feel the need to stretch a bit... Feeling guilty or wondering whether these tiny breaks may, in fact, be helpful?

Some research suggests that micro-breaks or short respite activities are helpful for momentarily undoing the negative effects (such as fatigue) that accrue from continuous, repetitive work. In fact, an intensive workday without respite opportunities makes recovering from the day's stress harder and makes its negative impacts persist through the evening. Engaging in micro-break activities voluntarily, between a series of tasks, is critical.

Micro-breaks that are beneficial for quick recovery comprise relaxation, nutrition-intake, and social or cognitive activities. A study by Kim and colleagues[55] showed that workers who engaged in relaxation activities (both physical and psychological, such as stretching, taking short walks, and listening to music) and social activities (socializing with coworkers for network matters or connecting with friends and significant others through conversations or texts) were more likely to recover momentarily from work stress. Such momentary recovery offsets the adverse effects of work stress at the end of the workday. However, in this study nutrition-intake (except for caffeine intake) and cognitive activities (e.g., reading newspapers or surfing the Internet) were not as effective in helping with momentary recovery from work demands and decreasing end-of-the-day negative effects.

So, as you write, today, consider these findings and observe your own patterns. Are you engaging in recovery tasks with your micro-breaks, or are you simply finding excuses to procrastinate? Identifying and managing the breaks you take, may become important strategies in managing your writing life.

---

[55] Kim, S., Park, Y., & Niu, Q. (2017). Micro-break activities at work to recover from daily work demands. *Journal of Organizational Behavior, 38*(1), 28-44.

SATURDAY
Week 11 - TIPS & TOOLS

Don't Break the Chain

I (MS) have tried different tools to help sustain my habit of writing every day. But, invariably, after a while I would get tired of a particular tool and stop using it. Many of these tools seemed to require extra effort and seemed only to add to my already-full workday. I either had to open an Excel file, carry a journal, or sign into a website (for which I would often forget my password!).

For the longest time, I was looking for something straightforward and "visual" to help keep track of my daily writing habit. Then, I learned about the "Don't Break the Chain" method while watching an episode of Seinfeld (yes, the TV comedy series).

The method entailed creating a table with all the dates for one semester, on a single page (of paper or screen). In the table, each row represented a week starting on a Monday and ending on a Sunday. If you don't want to create the table, use an empty calendar template – but it should have each week as a row. Then, I taped that single sheet of paper to my desk.

That was it! Only one page and I had to put an X on each cell/day that I wrote. The idea was never to break that chain of Xs.

The challenge of trying not to break the chain motivates you to sit down and write every day. It also drives you to continue, no matter what — because you really, really don't want to interrupt that beautiful string of Xs you are creating. Remember, if you don't write that day, you don't get to draw an X. It doesn't matter what you write about; it matters that you write something.

If you are interested in using an app on your phone or tablet, instead of paper, there are free apps for this tool, available for both IOS and PC platforms.

As soon as I finish writing this entry, I get to draw my X for today! Go start your chain, and see if you don't end up with a smile, happy you wrote something, anything… just not to break the chain.

SUNDAY
Week 11 - WRITING PROMPTS

Dear Editor

Not sure if this is true in your field, but scholars in the health sciences and medicine make interesting contributions by commenting on other scholars' publications. An appropriate venue for this is the "Letters to the Editor" section of traditional journals, or the space provided for readers to post comments about articles in open-access journals.

Although these comments can be extremely useful, because they suggest potential omissions, provide alternative findings, or raise important questions, they are difficult to write. The difficulty usually lies in striking the appropriate "tone" for the wording: Achieving the perfect balance between questioning or criticizing without attacking or demeaning.

So, today, try to locate one or two interesting letters to editors or comments posted to online journal articles. Deconstruct the letter or the comments into their main elements. Observe the choice of words and tone.

Then, try your hand at writing one of these. Don't worry about submitting it. For this exercise, you do not have to send it out at all. It's just for practice. However, if you feel you should submit it, give it your full attention and don't forget to apply all your editing skills. If you have an important question to raise, contrasting findings to offer, or are just plain glad to see someone tackle a forgotten topic, let the editor hear what you have to say. Remember that important contributions can be made in this fashion, given academic conversations are just that: Conversations carried out in a professional manner, within a professional venue.

Give it a try!

WEEK 12
Days 78 - 84

"My diploma has an expiration date. Apparently, I'm going to forget everything I learned by May, 2019."

MONDAY
Week 12 - BOOKS TO READ

Becoming an Academic Writer: 50 Exercises for Paced, Productive, and Powerful Writing [56]

I (PG) wrote the book, so it may seem like a conflict of interest to recommend it, here. I believe, however – based on the very positive and insightful feedback received over the years – the book can be helpful to many academic writers looking for a system to tackle their writing. You don't have to purchase it: Ask your library to do it.

Here is the book's structure: Part I contains exercises to establish a healthy and sustainable writing habit. In other words, how to develop a habit and maintain it (including support and motivation), alongside tips for structuring text and ensuring cohesion of the paragraphs, reside in exercises 1 through 28. Part II, or exercises 29 through 50, focuses on writing better introductions, methods, results and discussions in journal articles and/or research proposals. The Appendix describes how to read with a purpose and use a matrix to organize the readings and the information gleaned from them.

The lens through which I present the material is deep or deliberate practice. Deep practice is a feature that distinguishes mediocre performers from elite performers, according to research on the topic of talent or skill development. Deep practice is a special type of practice that requires one to establish an achievable goal for each practice session, slow down and pay attention while practicing, and obtain feedback, regularly.

Despite its anchor in deep practice, however, the book also touches on the issue of identity and challenges readers to view themselves as writers. We write for a living. We also conduct research, but the research is non-existent, if it's not communicated (in writing) to peers and to non-peers.

So… there's much to think about and to do when reading this book. It will put you to work, on a regular basis, with practice sessions that can last from a few minutes, to many writing sessions (if you so choose). If, therefore, you are looking for a toolbox and a system[57] (a set of procedures and tools) for your writing, take a look at the book.

And, if you feel so inclined, share your feedback with me. I (PG) would love to hear from you!

---

[56] Goodson, P. (2016). **Becoming an Academic Writer: 50 Exercises for Paced, Productive, and Powerful Writing** – 2nd edition. SAGE Publications.

[57] Check out the entry for **Tuesday, Week 11**, in this book, where we also talk about the need for a *system* to tackle academic writing.

TUESDAY
Week 12 - DEEP PRACTICE

Practicing Feedback

Just as you need to practice your writing – preferably using the principles of deep or deliberate practice (i.e., setting goals for each practice/writing session; slowing down to pay attention and be intentional) – you also need to practice getting-and-giving feedback. In fact, a feedback loop is an essential component of a deep or deliberate practice session. As you practice, you should stop the moment you detect an error, and begin again (at least that's the way instrument players are instructed to practice, if they follow a deep practice strategy).

We know… it's difficult to insert an immediate feedback loop (similar to 'hearing' a wrong note played on the piano) into our writing sessions, but obtaining feedback on our writing — regularly — is one way to do it.

BUT (and this is a big caveat): Obtaining useless or inappropriate feedback can be very damaging. Therefore, we need to learn and practice how to obtain (and give) the appropriate feedback for that particular 'moment' of the writing. It makes no sense to get feedback on grammar, if all you need is to know whether the idea is worth writing about in the first place (if it's not, who cares about grammar problems in the text?).

Today's challenge is this: For one of your current writing projects, decide in what stage of development is that piece. Then, ask yourself: What kind of feedback, at this moment, would be the most useful? In early stages of the writing project, reader-type feedback – the kind that merely assesses whether the idea is interesting or worth pursuing – is very helpful; in middle-stages, assessing how well the text is 'coming together' might be what you need (does it flow? Is it clear?); and in final stages of a writing project, nitty-gritty details need addressing (is the grammar correct? Are the sentences too long? Is the formatting following the instructions given to authors?).

After deciding what type of feedback would be most useful, select a small portion of the text for which to obtain feedback (don't overwhelm a feedback-giver with 30 pages of text, please!). Ask someone you know, who can give the type of feedback you need at this moment, for a 30-minute meeting to go over that small portion of the text and discuss the feedback you need. Feedback appointments like this make the feedback happen immediately; much better than having your text sit in someone's in-box for several weeks!

After trying this strategy (specific feedback on small portions of writing, obtained during a meeting), make it a point to practice this repeatedly, throughout the development of your writing project. Perhaps more importantly, still: Seek ways of providing this kind of targeted feedback to others around you, regularly. Practicing giving regular feedback on others' writing sometimes does more for improving the quality of your writing than getting feedback!

Give it a try and experience the difference this type of practice can make.

WEDNESDAY
Week 12 - HUMOR

"I know your career means everything to you, but couldn't you just marry me as a hobby?"

THURSDAY
Week 12 - INSPIRATION

Being Kind to a Rejected Paper

After I (MS) finished my PhD, I had a tough time getting my dissertation articles published. I received rejection emails, one after the other… Somewhere in the middle of that sea of rejection, my motivation and passion for those papers drowned.

After spending days feeling angry and overflowing with negativity due to one particular rejection, I decided to write a letter—a kind one—addressed to my rejected articles. My goal was to revive the passion I once had for them. I wanted to remind myself there were many positive elements in the papers, after all!

One of the letters, then, looks something like this…

Dear article,

Let me start by saying: I miss you. I know I have been unkind and avoided you for a while. I apologize. I am writing to touch base with you and see if we can work on our relationship; perhaps pick up where we left off?

Remember when I first drafted you, how excited we were? You and I knew we were onto something, were coming up with something unique and challenging (wasn't that an awesome feeling?!).

I must say I am proud of you and no amount of rejection can change how I feel about you. You have a carefully crafted purpose statement. You have a well-written introduction. You have interesting findings! I am thankful for the opportunity to have written you. And despite a disappointing final decision from the journal's editor, the reviewers DID have wonderful things to remark about you. [Here, I copied and pasted all the positive comments from reviewers].

So, I guess what's left is for us to spend some time together… Revising and sharing a good cup of coffee…

What's your schedule like this week?

Maybe you could write a similarly kind letter to a rejected manuscript that is sitting there, neglected (but screaming for attention) in your files. Think about your article as a person who needs some positive affirmation; purposefully, look for the compliments and positive comments reviewers provided. And think about yourself as a person who needs to practice being grateful for having had the opportunity to write.

Somehow, this simple (and apparently "silly") shift in focus sparked some of my lost motivation and had me working on those papers, once again.

And, yes: They did, in fact, get accepted! I'm so glad I didn't give up or give in…

Verbs

As academic writers, words are the essential tools of our craft. Academic writing, however, calls for a unique style of word choice: Precise and accurate with every word conveying the exact meaning it intends.

Frels, Onwuegbuzie and Slate[58] draw our attention to the verbs used in scholarly writing, and to their importance. The authors describe verbs as "vigorous, direct communicators." Yet, despite their power and function, some academic fields tend to overuse specific verbs. For example, "found" appears to be the most frequently used verb in the Social and Behavioral Sciences, according to these authors!

In the article we discuss here, the authors build on their (and other scholars') previous work analyzing academic writing, including analyses of the prevalence of specific mistakes in writing (in particular, those addressed in the Publication Manual of the American Psychological Association, or APA). They build on this previous work to develop their typology of verbs for scholarly writing – with the express purposes of alerting writers to the need for precision, as well as to provide useful alternatives to over-used verbs, such as "found".

After collecting and analyzing how academics use 195 specific verbs (sorted into 15 categories such as "evidence-based/data driven verbs", "explicit verbs", and "verification verbs") the authors propose their typology representing a) statement b) cognition, and c) knowledge or action verbs. For example, under the category "statement", authors list verbs such as "remarked, summed, and argued". Under the category "cognition", verbs such as "distinguished, ascertained, and attested" are listed. And, representing knowledge or action, they present verbs such as "encountered, scrutinized, and sampled" (see Tables 1 – 3 in the article for complete lists).

The proposed typology further categorizes verbs based on their strength from weak to strong according to their meaning. For example, among verbs useful for reporting a statement, 'indicate' would be weak, while 'declare' and 'pronounce' would be stronger. The article concludes by presenting lists of verbs appropriate for different sections of a journal article.

If you struggle with a narrow choice of verbs when you write, or you all of a sudden are "stuck" repeating the verb "found", over and over, you'll want to keep the list of verbs in this typology, handy. And because we are academics, observing how carefully the authors of these typology lists ground their work into a conceptual and evidence-based framework is nothing short of inspiring!

---

[58] Frels, R. K., Onwuegbuzie, A. J., & Slate, J. R. (2010). A Typology of Verbs for Scholarly Writing. *Research in the Schools, 17*(1), xx-xxxi.

SATURDAY
Week 12 - TIPS & TOOLS

Panda Planner[59]

I (MS) had never been a fan of planners until a good friend introduced me to the Panda Planner. I specifically like the story behind the product:

The creator of the Panda Planner, Michael Leip, was dealt a couple of serious blows in his life: First, a Traumatic Brain Injury (TBI) and, later, cancer. These conditions landed Michael in the midst of depression, anxiety, and the inability to think clearly. When he was able to get back on track, he searched for a system to help overcome his difficulties and increase the productivity he needed as a self-employed entrepreneur. After reading several books and journal articles, he created his version of a planning system, which became the Panda Planner.

The Panda Planner aims to provide a system to motivate and inspire its users (you) to fulfill their life goals, be more productive, and feel happier. The Planner has three major sections for monthly, weekly, and daily planning. Leip designed the planner's main features based on principles of positive psychology to help users focus on what has been accomplished and how to improve (e.g., 'big wins,' 'things I will do to make this week great'). Below are some of the features designed to help users (you?) be more productive:

The weekly planning section reviews last week's 'big wins' and captures ideas for 'how to improve' in the upcoming week.

Each daily planning page has a designated area to list each day's priorities. The list of priorities functions as a constant reminder of the important tasks that will help achieve your goals for the week. Writing is the number one priority on this list, for me.

The Panda Planer encourages you to begin the day with a positive review of what you are excited about and what you are grateful for. Also, defining a focus for the day and an affirmation will keep you motivated and inspired.

There is a designated portion of the daily planning page to set aside a list of tasks. This allows you to distinguish between priorities and other necessary things to do (but are not priorities). You can accumulate the tasks on your list and then get them done all at once instead of letting them interfere with the time dedicated to your priorities.

Ending the day with a nightly review of 'wins' and 'areas for improvement' diminishes the feeling of guilt if you did not spend time on your important goals.

There are several versions of the planner available, and most versions are not dated, so you can begin using at any moment. Some versions even have online support to help enhance your productivity in a positive manner. Give it a try!

---

[59] There are several other planners available, which seek to achieve similar goals as the Panda Planner. We encourage you to find one that you like and try it out. The Panda Planner happens to be a resource we know and can recommend. The planner is available at https://pandaplanner.com, Amazon and Etsy.

SUNDAY
Week 12 - WRITING PROMPTS

Questioning Assumptions

One of the most important contributions academics can make to knowledge-building is a contribution to the theories in one's field. Theories are narratives (or stories) crafted to explain phenomena using abstractions, concepts, constructs and the relationships these constructs have with each other.

All theories rest on certain assumptions: Those values, beliefs, statements-of-fact that are not questioned or tested. They are accepted by all as valid or true.

But theories are also products of their times and their creators (who are, too, a product of their times). Therefore, the assumptions that underlie scientific theories can and do change, over time.

Today, think of a theory in your field. One with which you are familiar and have used in your work. If needed, go back to one or two of the classical writings about the theory to remind yourself of what it proposed.

Now: Challenge yourself to question one of its basic assumptions, in writing. Even if just to write a single question about that assumption. Keep it short. Keep it simple.

For example: Most theories explaining how people choose between healthy/unhealthy behaviors are based on a value-expectancy assumption. This assumption presupposes that human beings weigh the pros and cons of a behavior before choosing a course of action (e.g., when deciding whether to eat a doughnut every night after supper I contrast how much I really, really want it with how much I really, really would like not to gain weight or become a diabetic). Based on this assumption, most theories will come up with concepts/constructs that explain how this decision is made and which factors can be tweaked to affect the decision (in a positive or negative direction).

This notion, however, that people make decisions by weighing the pros and cons is an assumption. A belief most theories take for granted and don't test. If I were to begin questioning this assumption, I would probably write something like this: "Health behavior theories are anchored on the assumption that people make decisions about their health by weighing the pros and cons of the behavior, and decide in favor of the most positive outcome. This assumption presupposes people make decisions rationally. It doesn't seem to take into account any emotional, intuitive, or sub-conscious mechanisms that probably play an important role in decision-making. I wonder if anyone has questioned this assumption, before."

You may not have much to say about the assumption, but just asking the questions — "Is this assumption valid? Is it universally applicable? Should this assumption be checked out?" — might get your thinking tuned in to some really interesting questions you might ask about the status quo in your field. You will probably begin to have some very interesting and provocative ideas for your next research project.

Give it a try!

WEEK 13
Days 85 - 90

MONDAY
Week 13 - BOOKS TO READ

Professors as Writers: A Self-Help Guide To Productive Writing [60]

Why recommend a book that is three decades old? Because, unfortunately, much of what Robert Boice highlighted as problems academics face regarding writing remains unchanged. Professors still struggle to view themselves as writers, and continue to battle many personal obstacles when writing and publishing. Despite its dated age, therefore, Boice's work remains both timely and timeless.

Boice begins the book addressing the issue, "Why Professors Don't Write" (Chapter 1), and proceeds offering strategies for both short-term solutions and long-term growth. His main emphasis: Separating the processes of generating and editing text.

As a scholar who dedicated much of his time to exploring reasons why academic writers become blocked — not writing at all, or not writing as much as they could — Boice explores throughout the book the various reasons leading to "writers' block" and offering solutions readers can begin implementing immediately. He proposes, for instance, four steps to facilitate "writing without blocking": (1) automaticity; (2) externality; (3) self-control, and (4) sociality.

From his perspective, automaticity leads to generating text in a manner that is free from internal censors and builds the writer's confidence; externality refers to controlling external contingencies; self-control, here, refers to "control over one's consciousness, especially over its tendencies to distortion and negativism" (p.98); and sociality is the attempt to avoid isolation, while obtaining feedback and encouragement for one's writing.

As useful as Boice's approach is – as a whole – some might say the most useful portion of his book lies in the Appendix Part 1. Here, Boice appended "The Blocking Questionnaire: An Instrument for Assessing Writing Problems". This is an invaluable self-assessment tool, capable of providing valuable insights into ourselves, as writers. Completing the questions and then using the scores obtained to identify which problems, in particular, need our attention or could improve, represents a large step in the direction of knowing our writer-selves better and improving.

The tools and insights Robert Boice provided the academic community regarding their writing remain as valuable as they were when he first introduced the topic. We strongly recommend the book and the Questionnaire as invaluable tools for growing as an academic writer. Check it out!

---

[60] Boice, R. (1990). **Professors as Writers: A Self-Help Guide to Productive Writing**. New Forums Press.

TUESDAY
Week 13 - DEEP PRACTICE

A 30-Day Writing Challenge

There's something about watching other people push themselves to their limit. Watching the Olympics, for instance: As the hope of victory builds and athletes' herculean efforts amaze, the promise of glory seduces, allures. Suddenly, we are motivated – we want to be like that, we want to do that! We, too, want to test our limits, push ourselves, see how far we can possibly go. Getting a medal in the process may not be so bad, either, we think; even just a pat on the back for effort, might do.

One of my (PG) colleagues runs ultra-marathons (distances ranging between 31 and 100 miles, sometimes, more). His name is Mike. I am truly inspired by Mike's achievements: I want to be like him, I want to do that, too!

Just one tiny problem: I don't run. I hate running. Never liked it, seems like I never will (despite serious efforts to learn, years ago). So, I'll never do that. Yet, the way Mike approaches running inspires me. The way he pushes himself to the limit moves me and makes me ask: Can I be like him?

The answer, of course, is yes! Specifically, what I have learned from Mike is how to approach herculean tasks such as 100 mile-races, or those insurmountable writing projects. "You do it one mile-at-a-time," he says; "you take the whole race and break it down to one day at a time." You plan it in reasonable, achievable "chunks", you stay with it, day-after-day, monitor-and-adjust your responses continually, and focus only on the day ahead (not on the 99 miles left to go).

I applied the principle to my writing. No, I didn't embark on an ultra-marathon of writing a novel in 30 days – although there are people and resources dedicated to achieving precisely that feat[61]. An ultra-marathon of writing would go against the principle of avoiding binge-writing and engaging in it slowly, but steadily.

Instead, I gave myself a small challenge: To write 1 page of new words every day, for 30 days on a specific project. They didn't have to be coherent, structured, or meaningful – the words, not the days. They could be just ideas I had about the project, notions I wished to explore further, possible arguments, lists of people I needed to search, books and films I needed to check out. Anything related to that project. At day 30, I had 70 pages of text, single-spaced.

Did I push myself to the limit? Not really… but I silenced my inner critic who kept insisting I couldn't possibly generate text related to that specific project, especially while I was still analyzing data and didn't have any findings to report. The challenge kept me moving, generating new words, writing daily, maturing new ideas, exploring old ones.

I must confess, though: I had a lot of fun writing and, when I finished and looked back at what I had accomplished, decided: I want to do that again, continue to be like that, continue to test my limits, even if I won't win a gold medal for any of it! (I must write Mike a note of thanks…). How about you? Why not set a mini-challenge and see what you can achieve?

---

[61] Check out the **Nanowrimo Young Writers' Program** online: https://ywp.nanowrimo.org/

WEDNESDAY
Week 13 - HUMOR

To-Do: A List for Writers Preparing (Not) to Write

1. Make sure you have checked the fridge one last time; there is always something hidden somewhere that you might have missed the previous nineteen times you searched.
2. Don't forget to tackle that under-the-sofa stain, which has been there for four and a half years.
3. Keep the tweezers next to the computer; that nasty hair under your chin makes you look terrible!
4. Check your social media notifications one last time (promise it will be the last time, for the next 15 minutes); *this* Facebook notification might be from your potential employer.
5. Your emails pile up if you don't keep checking; handle them as they come in.
6. What is this oddly-shaped nail? Keep the nail file next to the tweezers.
7. Take two seconds to order that vitamin D supplement, whose purchase you keep forgetting.
8. Browse that brochure that has been sitting on the kitchen table for 7 days; it's waited too long for your attention.
9. Pay the utilities bill now; you will forget it later.
10. Do the dishes, quickly; the coffee at the bottom of the cups sitting in the sink is growing mouldy (after all, it's been there for at least 45 minutes!!!).
11. (Add to this list any other item you've been procrastinating taking action on for the last 5 years).

THURSDAY
Week 13 - INSPIRATION

Accomplishments List

We know all about lists: To-do, assignments, birthdays, Christmas cards, places to visit before we die ("bucket"), phone numbers, pros-and-cons, the list in yesterday's entry of this book (see the previous page), and many others. We know how they help us remember, provide structure to our tasks, scaffold our memories. If you've read the book "The Checklist Manifesto"[62] by Atul Gawande, you've also learned the importance of check-lists for the minimizing errors during surgeries, preventing infections in hospitals, and flying airplanes. (If you haven't yet read the book, go take a look; it's really interesting!).

Yet, despite our knowledge and personal use, we rarely think about developing an "Accomplishments" or a "Have-Done" list. Reasons vary for neglecting this useful tool: From thinking that merely crossing off the "to-do" list signifies "completed task" and, therefore, no need for a further step, to "Oh, no! Another list?!?!?"

The latter used to be my (PG) excuse for not developing a list of accomplishments until one day, when I had reached the end of a semester that felt particularly hectic. I simply couldn't pin-point what I had done. I was exhausted, feeling like I had not achieved "enough", but couldn't see the fruit of my labor. That's when I decided to begin a list of things I had accomplished, finished, or set in motion. I began to lay out all the tangible items from the old crossed out to-do lists, adding those intangible accomplishments such as "did not snap at Charlie, even once, during our monthly meetings!".

I have turned this little task into something I routinely perform every end-of-semester and end-of-the-year. And: I have them together, in one place (with their respective dates, obviously), so I can – at a glance – view the bulk of my accomplishments. I can't begin to describe how affirming and validating these lists have been – true and faithful "reality checks". I often find that I accomplished much, much more than I can recall!

So, today, think about developing your own list of accomplishments. Choose a specific time-period (it can be for last week or last month or last semester; it can be for your whole career – although starting with a narrower focus tends to be more concrete and practical). Refer to your planner, calendar or old to-do lists and begin jotting down all your accomplishments. Refer to these lists when you feel discouraged or defeated; when doubts about your abilities come to haunt you, there's the evidence that your negative views are unrealistic. If anyone doubts you, show them the evidence!

Give it a try!

Oh… and don't forget to add "Started accomplishments list on (date)…".

---

[62] Gawande, A. (2011). **The Checklist Manifesto: How to Get Things Right.** Picador.

FRIDAY
Week 13 - RESEARCH

Writing About Your Goals Works! [63]

Edwin A. Locke and Gary P. Latham are known for having developed Goal-Setting Theory (GST). They developed GST, at first, through an induction process based on approximately 400 scholarly studies. This inductive process helped establish the theory's main constructs, mediators, and moderators. Over time, the authors refined the theory's main constructs, its mediators and moderators, through the contribution of several authors conducting research on goal-setting. In the brief article we review, here, Locke reflects on research regarding the effectiveness of writing about one's goals, and claims boldly: "Writing about your goals works."

Locke refers, for instance, to the work of Cheryl Travers[64], a researcher in the UK, who has been studying goal-setting for several years. Travers leads a program that requires students to write extensively about their goals in life. The program seems to help students improve their lives in many ways, although outcomes have not been measured. In another example, Locke describes the study by Morisano, Hirsh, Peterson, Pihl and Shore[65], which used a computer program and required college students to discuss their ideal futures (personal life goals) for two hours. The researchers measured students' performance outcomes and showed students who wrote about their goals (grade goals or even other goals) had better academic performance compared to students in a control group.

To these descriptions of specific studies, Locke adds his insight about the mechanisms through which writing about goals affects action. He proposes that writing (1) objectifies and clarifies goals and values and (2) brings ideas from the subconscious realm into the conscious (Locke has conducted important research on the role of subconscious goals). Both features increase a person's commitment to action and improves a person's self-efficacy, especially if the writing incorporates tangible action steps.

So... Does it really work? There seems to be something to it. How about conducting an experiment (N=1), and verifying the answer yourself? Compare two weeks in which you write down your goals, to two other weeks in which you skip that step. Who knows? You may have enough valuable data to report on a case study, yourself!

---

[63] Locke, E. A. (2019). What Makes Writing about Goals Work? *Academy of Management Discoveries, 5* (2), 109-110. Online only: https://doi.org/10.5465/amd.2018.0187

[64] Travers, C. J. 2013. *Using goal setting theory to promote personal development*. In E. A. Locke & G. P. Latham (Eds.), **New developments in goal setting and task performance**. Routledge.

[65] Morisano, D., Hirsh, J. B., Petersen, J. B., Pihl, R. O., & Shore, B. M. 2010. Setting, elaborating, and reflecting on personal goals improves academic performance. *Journal of Applied Psychology, 95*: 255–264.

SATURDAY
Week 13 - TIPS & TOOLS

De-Jargonizer

You know this: When writing for lay audiences about your research/scholarship, you need to "tone down" the specialized language, the technical terms. Yes, you do know that, but the gulf between knowing and acting is, oftentimes, magnified because you just can't see where the specialized, technical language is. You are fish-in-water, when it comes to writing on topics with which you're familiar.

Any tool (or other person) who can point out to you where the technical terms are, can be tremendously helpful. If these problem-spots are highlighted, then you can decide whether the term is absolutely essential to keep in the text (and you may need to provide an explanation somewhere), or if it can be changed to a more common term.

Enter: the De-Jargonizer tool, available at: http://scienceandpublic.com. To use the tool, you simply upload the text you want analyzed (or copy and paste it manually into the text box) and it will run an analysis, presenting some of the findings color-coded. The "Instructions" tab at the very top of the first page will tell you precisely what to do and what to expect. Another tab leads you to "examples". It will color, in your text, the words that are common (in black), those that are used with mid-frequency (in orange), and jargon (or rare) words (in red).

The tool was developed by a team of professors and students (in Science Communication, in Humanities and Arts, in Applied Mathematics and in Computer Science) at the Technion – Israel Institute of Technology (the tab "Developers" gives you their names and affiliations). The developers also present their rationale for developing the tool and a portion of the literature informing their work. In addition, they offer a brief summary of what the literature judges as acceptable amounts of jargon/technical or unknown terms in a text, when communicating with lay audiences.

Even if you're not writing about scientific topics for lay audiences, it is useful to bear in mind something the authors of the De-Jargonizer mention: "Studies have shown that a reader needs to understand 98% of vocabulary in a text to adequately comprehend the content …"

Do your readers, in fact, understand 98% of what you write? Are you sure ?